CONTENTS

1

Build your own Deck?

The answer is YES! By doing the planning and all or part of the work yourself, you can have the deck you might not otherwise be able to afford. By supplying the labor and buying materials yourself, construction costs can be cut significantly.

Framing out a deck is not difficult. Standardized materials and construction techniques make it relatively easy if you take time to plan and work carefully.

Planning your Deck

The key to a successful deck project is planning, planning, and more planning! Once you have begun construction of your deck, it is both costly and time-consuming to correct errors in deck placement, construction, or selection of materials. So the motto of the Do-It-Yourself deck builder must be **PLAN AHEAD!** Whether you choose to draw the plans for your deck following the guidelines in this manual or you decide to purchase a *UCANDO* deck plan which can be adapted to your unique requirements, you must carefully plan all elements of your deck project.

Here is a checklist of design information which you must gather *before* you begin to design your deck:

Local Building Requirements. Visit your local building department and determine how local building codes and zoning ordinances will influence your project. Be prepared to apply for a building permit once you have completed your design.

Deed Restrictions. Are there conditions in your property deed that restrict the type and location of your deck? Are you planning to place your deck over property controlled by an easement for right-of-way or utility access?

Climatic Factors. You need to determine specific climatic conditions on your property. For example, what is the maximum soil frost depth at your site? What is the prevailing wind direction during the season when your deck will receive maximum use? How much snow load will your deck have to carry during the winter months? Finally, evaluate the microclimate of your intended deck location. Microclimate includes the shading effects of deciduous or evergreen trees and shrubs, the angle of the sun in relation to nearby landscaping during different seasons, soil drainage conditions, and prevailing wind and temperature conditions.

Deck Functions. What do you want your deck to do? Will your deck serve as an extension of a room in your home? Do you see your deck as a social gathering spot or as a place of seclusion from your neighbors? Do you want your deck to perform a special function such as containing a built-in barbecue or supporting a portable spa or hot tub?

All the techniques and tips you'll need are in this book. Read it carefully before you begin construction. It will help you determine the work you can handle alone and also where expert help might be needed to do the job right.

You can also learn many construction basics by studying existing decks. Ask your neighbors if you can take a few minutes to review their decks before you begin planning your design.

Your Budget. You must determine an estimated dollar amount that you plan to spend on your deck. Do you plan to construct the deck yourself or will you subcontract with a professional to build the deck after you have purchased materials? Perhaps you want a contractor to complete your deck project in its entirety. It is helpful if you can set upper and lower spending limits so that you can consider options in the materials that you plan for your deck. If you decide to finance your deck project, don't forget to include interest cost in the total cost amount.

Your Materials Source. While many of you will shop different sources for materials after you have completed your design work and settled on a bill of materials, you should remember that a helpful lumber dealer or home center is an invaluable resource for the successful completion of your deck project. Consult with a dealer of your choice to be certain that they stock all the materials you require. If special ordering is necessary, determine lead times for the materials that the dealer does not carry in regular inventory. Check if the dealer can deliver materials directly to your site. Don't underestimate the importance of a reputable dealer in providing both quality materials and design knowledge.

Planning Your Deck   Continued

The deck site plans on this page are included to exemplify how your deck can serve as an extension of the living space in your home. Consider first how you want to access your deck--which rooms in particular should provide entry to your deck space. Do you currently have enough door openings to handle the traffic on your deck? Perhaps you need to install additional patio doors to provide more than one access point.

If you are planning a deck which is attached to your home, you must carefully evaluate the use of door and window openings to integrate the deck with your home. Multiple access points open your deck to the interior living space of your home. For example, Figure 3-A illustrates a wraparound deck which you can access from the dining room or the sun room area.

Decks provide a sense of openness to the living space of your home. However, you can also create an enclosed, private environment with a deck that adjoins two exterior walls. In Figure 3-B, observe how the modest rectangular deck links the living room and the family room while the walls of those rooms provide protection from the elements and privacy.

If you are fortunate enough to be able to construct a large deck like those illustrated in Figures 3-C and 3-D, you will increase the total usable living area of your home significantly by careful planning and deck design. These decks add extremely useful square footage which can serve multiple functions--a simple recreation space, an outdoor dining and entertainment area, or happily a place to get away and relax.

Figure 3-A

Figure 3-B

Figure 3-C

Figure 3-D

A Decision Guide for Designing your Deck

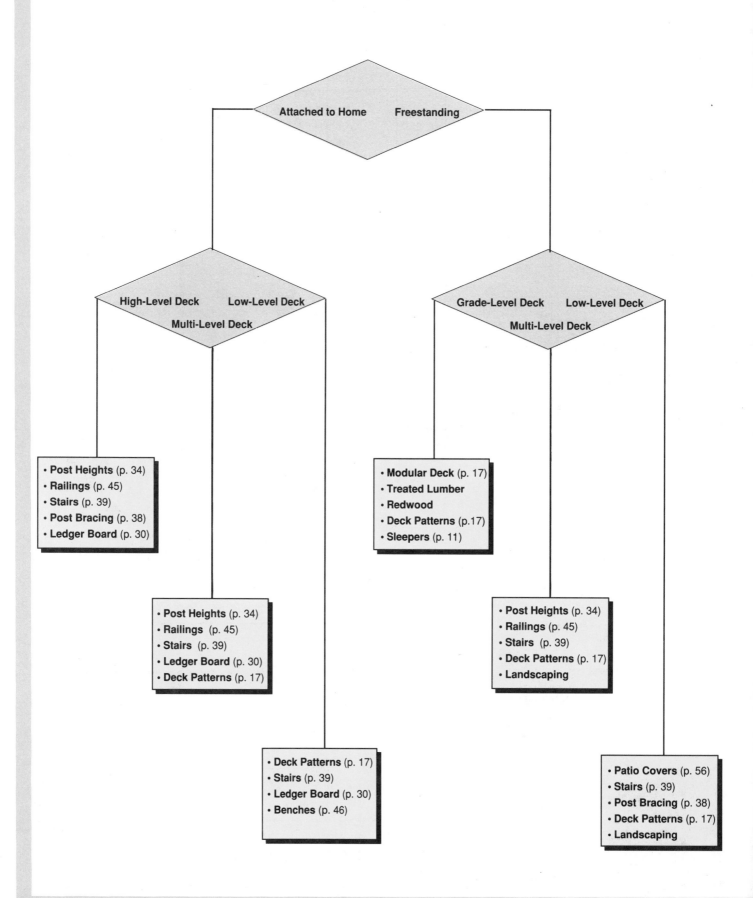

Attached to Home   Freestanding

High-Level Deck   Low-Level Deck

Multi-Level Deck

Grade-Level Deck   Low-Level Deck

Multi-Level Deck

• **Post Heights** (p. 34)
• **Railings** (p. 45)
• **Stairs** (p. 39)
• **Post Bracing** (p. 38)
• **Ledger Board** (p. 30)

• **Modular Deck** (p. 17)
• **Treated Lumber**
• **Redwood**
• **Deck Patterns** (p.17)
• **Sleepers** (p. 11)

• **Post Heights** (p. 34)
• **Railings** (p. 45)
• **Stairs** (p. 39)
• **Ledger Board** (p. 30)
• **Deck Patterns** (p. 17)

• **Post Heights** (p. 34)
• **Railings** (p. 45)
• **Stairs** (p. 39)
• **Deck Patterns** (p. 17)
• **Landscaping**

• **Deck Patterns** (p. 17)
• **Stairs** (p. 39)
• **Ledger Board** (p. 30)
• **Benches** (p. 46)

• **Patio Covers** (p. 56)
• **Stairs** (p. 39)
• **Post Bracing** (p. 38)
• **Deck Patterns** (p. 17)
• **Landscaping**

A Buyer's Guide to *UCANDO* Plans and Templates

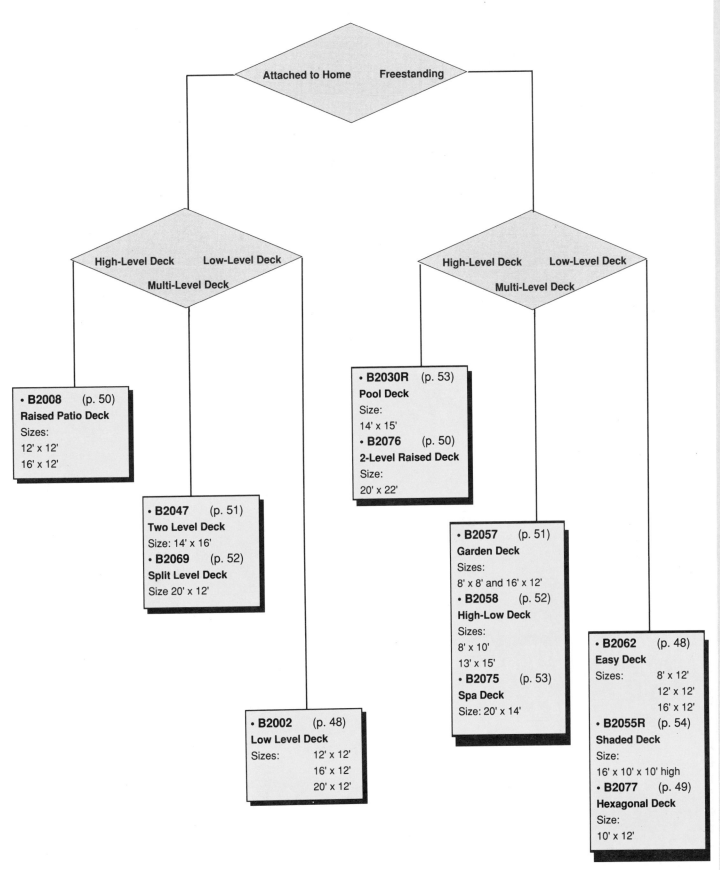

Attached to Home — Freestanding

High-Level Deck — Low-Level Deck
Multi-Level Deck

High-Level Deck — Low-Level Deck
Multi-Level Deck

• **B2008** (p. 50)
Raised Patio Deck
Sizes:
12' x 12'
16' x 12'

• **B2047** (p. 51)
Two Level Deck
Size: 14' x 16'
• **B2069** (p. 52)
Split Level Deck
Size 20' x 12'

• **B2002** (p. 48)
Low Level Deck
Sizes: 12' x 12'
16' x 12'
20' x 12'

• **B2030R** (p. 53)
Pool Deck
Size:
14' x 15'
• **B2076** (p. 50)
2-Level Raised Deck
Size:
20' x 22'

• **B2057** (p. 51)
Garden Deck
Sizes:
8' x 8' and 16' x 12'
• **B2058** (p. 52)
High-Low Deck
Sizes:
8' x 10'
13' x 15'
• **B2075** (p. 53)
Spa Deck
Size: 20' x 14'

• **B2062** (p. 48)
Easy Deck
Sizes: 8' x 12'
12' x 12'
16' x 12'
• **B2055R** (p. 54)
Shaded Deck
Size:
16' x 10' x 10' high
• **B2077** (p. 49)
Hexagonal Deck
Size:
10' x 12'

See pages 48-64 for Additional Information.

For Notes and Layout Procedures...

¹/₄"=1'-0" Scale

For Notes and Layout Procedures...

For Notes and Layout Procedures...

¹/4"=1'-0" Scale

ANATOMY OF A DECK

2" x 6" Decking

2-2" x 4" Trim Boards

Optional Stair
2-2" x 6" Stair Treads
2" x 6" Stair Carriage (48" O.C. max.)
Anchored to Concrete Pad

Clip
Angles

Bench

2" x 4" with $\frac{1}{4}$ Spacing
Porch Deck

Metal Joist Hangers

2" x 8"

1" x 4" Trim Board

3-2" x 4"

2-2" x 8" Wood Beams

2" x 12" Stringer

Metal Anchor
12" Dia.
Concrete Pier

STANDARD LEVEL DECK

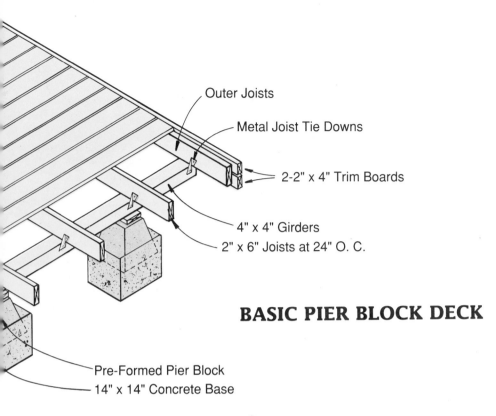

Outer Joists

Metal Joist Tie Downs

2-2" x 4" Trim Boards

4" x 4" Girders

2" x 6" Joists at 24" O. C.

BASIC PIER BLOCK DECK

Pre-Formed Pier Block

14" x 14" Concrete Base

2" x 6" Decking Laid Flat ¼ Spacing

2" x 8" @ 24" O.C. Floor Joists

Metal Joist Hangers

2" x 8" Ledger

Framing Anchor

2" x 10" Stringer

2" x 10" Treads

2" x 10" Skirt Board

2-2" x 8" Beam

4" x 4" Wood Post

Clip Angles

Metal Anchor
12" Dia. Concrete Pier

Concrete Pad

RAISED DECK

Deck Glossary (A to M)

Anchor. Any metal connector device which is placed in wet concrete and helps to secure posts to piers.

Baluster. A vertical railing member typically cut from 2x2 stock that spans top and bottom rails.

Batterboard. Scrap lumber nailed horizontally to stakes driven near each corner of the deck excavation. Stretch nylon strings between batterboards to transfer reference points and to measure elevation.

Beam. Beams are horizontal structural members that are supported by vertical posts. Beams can support joist members on end or decking can be placed directly on beams in certain designs. Typically constructed from 2 or more 2-bys or 4-by material. See beam span chart for allowable beam spacing and spans. Also called a girder.

Blocking. Material cut from same stock as joist members and nailed between joists for horizontal stability.

Bracing. Bracing provides vertical stability to post members on high-level decks. Diagonal bracing should be lag bolted to connecting members for extra stability.

Bridging. Wood or metal cross pieces fastened between joists to provide structural strength and stability.

Cantilever. Refers to the end portion of a joist or the entire portion of the deck that extends beyond the beam.

Cap Rail. The cap rail is the topmost horizontal railing piece of deck railing. Typically 2x6 or 2x4.

Cleat. A short nailer which supports decking or stair treads.

Codes. Regulations implemented by your local building department which control the design and construction of buildings and other structures such as decks. Consult your local building department for applicable codes *before* you begin to build your deck.

Deck Board Tie. A metal fastener which allows you to fasten decking to joists without using nails visible on the surface of the decking. See page 43.

Deck Screws. A thin-shanked self-drilling screw which is a superior fastener for attaching decking. Especially useful in climates where decking boards must be removed and replaced due to severe weathering.

Decking. Typically 2x4, 2x6, or $5/4$" radius edged lumber placed flatwise on 16" or 24" spaced joists. Decking is available in many wood species and grades. Choose your decking material carefully because decking determines the final appearance and durability of your completed deck.

Defect. Any defect in lumber whether as a result of a manufacturing imperfection or an irregularity in the timber from which the lumber was cut. Some defects are only blemishes while others can reduce strength and durability. Grading rules establish the extent and severity of wood defects.

Edge. The narrowest side of a piece of lumber which is perpendicular to both the face and the end.

Elevation. Drawing of your deck design as it will appear from the front, rear, left and right sides.

Face. The widest side of a piece of lumber which is perpendicular to both the edge and the end.

Finish. Any protective coating applied to your deck to protect against weathering. Deck finishes are available as stains, paints, or preservatives.

Footing. Concrete footings help to anchor your piers in the surrounding soil and distribute weight over a larger surface area. In climates where the soil freezes, a generous footing protects against soil heaves and movement of your deck.

Frost Line. Measure of the maximum penetration of frost in the soil in a given geographic location. Depth of frost penetration varies with climate conditions.

Galvanized Nails. Hot-dipped galvanized nails (HDG) are dipped in zinc and will not rust.

Girder. Same as beam.

Grade Stamp. A stamp imprinted on dimensional lumber which identifies wood species, grade, texture, moisture content, and usage. Grade descriptions such as select, finish, and common signify limiting characteristics that may occur in lumber in each grade. The stamp indicates a uniform measurement of performance that permits lumber of a given grade to be used for the same purpose, regardless of the manufacturer.

Grading. The process of excavating, leveling, and compacting the soil or gravel beneath your deck to its desired finish level. Proper grading avoids drainage problems under your completed deck.

Grain. Lumber shows either a flat or vertical grain depending on how it was cut from the log. To minimize warping along the face of decking (known as cupping) and raising of the grain, you should place flat grain decking with the bark side up or facing out.

Gravel. Granular rock material that varies in size from approximately $1/4$" to 3" in diameter. Results from either natural disintegration of stone or crushing and processing of rock.

Heartwood. Core of the log that resists decay.

Joist. Typically 2-by lumber which is set on edge and supports your decking. Joists in turn are supported by beams, ledgers, and rim joists. See joist span chart on page 15 for maximum allowable joist spacing and spans for a given joist size.

Joist hanger. A metal connector available in many sizes and styles that attaches to a ledger or rim joist and makes a secure butt joint between ledger and joist.

Lag Screw. Heavy-duty fastener with hexagonal bolt head that provides extra fastening power for railing posts, ledgers, and other critical structural connections. Use galvanized lag screws and washers to prevent rust.

Ledger. The ledger board is attached with lag screws to the side of your house in attached deck construction. The ledger supports joists which are attached to the ledger with joist hangers.

Live Load. The predetermined load that a deck is capable of supporting expressed in pounds per square foot. Live load includes moving and variable loads such as people, furniture, or portable spas.

Metal Connectors. Used to augment or replace nails as fasteners, metal connectors are critical for lasting and sturdy deck construction.

Deck Glossary (M to Z)

Moisture Content. Moisture content of wood is the weight of water in wood expressed as a percentage of the weight of wood from which all water has been removed. The drier the lumber the less the lumber will shrink and warp on your finished deck. Surfaced lumber with a moisture content of 19% or less is known as dry lumber and is typically grade stamped as "S-DRY." Moisture content over 19% results in a "S-GRN" stamp to indicate surfaced green. Avoid green lumber especially when selecting your decking boards.

Pea Gravel. Approximately 1/4" round gravel material which can be used in a 4"-6" layer to cover the soil under your deck. Provides drainage and prevents soil-to-wood contact for decks built on sleepers rather than piers.

Perimeter. Outside boundary of the deck structure.

Perpendicular. At a 90 degree or right angle.

Pier. Piers support the total weight load of your deck and anchor the deck to the soil. Concrete piers can either be precast in a pyramidal shape with a nailing block on top or poured in place. Precast piers are typically used in climates where the soil does not freeze hard. Poured in place piers are utilized where the soil freezes and must extend a certain depth below the frost line. Either precast or poured in place piers should have adequate footings to prevent movement of the pier in the soil. Consult your local building department for requirements regarding pier type and placement.

Pilot Hole. A slightly undersized hole drilled in lumber which prevents splitting of the wood when nailed .

Plumb. Absolutely vertical. Determined with either a plumb bob or spirit level.

Post. The vertical support which bears the weight of the joists and attached decking. Typically posts are at least 4x4 lumber. When post height exceeds a limit defined by your local building code, posts must be stabilized by bracing. Vertical railing supports are also known as posts.

Pressure-Treated. Refers to the process of forcing preservative compounds into the fibre of the wood. Handle pressure-treated lumber with caution and do not inhale or burn its sawdust. Certain types of pressure-treated lumber are suitable for ground contact use while others must be used above ground. While more expensive than untreated lumber, pressure-treated wood resists decay and is recommended where naturally decay-resistant species like cedar or redwood are unavailable or too costly.

Rail. Any horizontal railing member.

Redwood. Decay-resistant and stable wood for long-lasting deck construction. Redwood grades from best to worst are: Clear All Heart (no knots), Construction Heart (small knots), Construction Common (sapwood), Merchantable Heart (knots and knotholes), and Merchantable (sapwood with knots and knotholes). Heart grades provide the greatest decay resistance.

Reinforcing Bar. A steel rod which provides internal reinforcement for concrete piers. Also known as rebar.

Right Triangle, 3-4-5. A means of ensuring squareness when you lay out your deck. Mark a vertical line at exactly 4'-0" from the angle you want to square. Then mark a horizontal line at exactly 3'-0" from the crossing vertical line. Measure the distance diagonally between both the 3' and 4' marks and when the distance measures exactly 5'-0" you have squared a 90 degree angle between lines.

Rim Joist. A perimeter joist to which the deck joists are attached.

Rise. Refers to the vertical height between each step in stair construction.

Sapwood. Outer layers of growth between the bark and heartwood. Less decay-resistant than heartwood.

Scale. A system of representation in plan drawing where small dimensions represent an equivalent large dimension. In typical deck plans the drawings are said to be scaled down. Scale is expressed as an equation such as 1/4"=1'-0".

Sleeper. Typically a decay-resistant 4x4 member which is placed horizontally on the ground or gravel bed and which supports decking. Recommended use is only in dry climates with stable soil.

Slope. A measurement of ground inclination and expressed as a percentage of units of vertical rise per 100 units of horizontal distance.

Spacing. In deck construction the distance between joist members and measured from center to center.

Span. The distance between beam supports which is measured center to center.

Spirit Level. A sealed cylinder with a transparent tube nearly filled with liquid forming a bubble used to indicate true vertical and horizontal alignment when the bubble is centered in the length of the tube.

Stair stringer. An inclined 2-by member that supports the treads of a stair. Stringers can be notched with a template pattern or unnotched where treads are supported with metal step support brackets. Also known as carriage or riser.

Step support. Step supports are 10 1/4" or 8 1/4" long specially configured brackets made from 12 gauge galvanized structural grade steel. They make it easier to build stairs when it is necessary to adjust the angle of the stringers to span the distance between the deck and the ground.

String Level. A spirit level mounted in a frame with prongs at either end for hanging on a string. Determines level across string lines.

Texture. Refers to the surface finish of lumber.

Tread. Treads provide the horizontal stepping surface in stair construction. To ensure against tread breakage, use clear 2-by wood without knots for treads.

Trim Board. A nonstructural board that covers the ends of decking boards or is abutted to the rim joist. To prevent warping, you can attach trim boards with screws.

Toenail. To drive a nail at an angle. When you toenail a post to a beam for example, you should drive the nail so that one-half the nail is in each member.

Zinc-Coated. Refers to fasteners coated with zinc, a non-corrosive metal used as a galvanizing material.

Drawing a Plan for Your Deck

Obtain the Correct Drawing Tools. The tools you will need to draw plans for your deck are available at your local stationery or variety store. You should obtain a **transparent plastic ruler** to help you keep your drawings to scale. **Scale** is a system of representation in plan drawing where small dimensions represent an equivalent large dimension. Scale is typically expressed as an equation such as $1/4"=1'-0"$. Better than a simple ruler is an **architect's scale** which calibrates dimensions directly to the scale used on your drawing. You can read 5'-0" at $1/4"$ scale directly on the architect's scale rather than multiplying $5 \times 1/4" = 1\ 1/4"$ and measuring to scale with your ruler.

Also purchase two **transparent right angle triangles** which help to measure angles and keep your work square. You should obtain a 6" 45 degree triangle and a 6" 30/60 degree triangle. Use a medium lead pencil to draw your plans and have a rubber eraser at hand—you will need it to correct inevitable revisions. We have provided graph paper in this manual at two different scales for your convenience. Finally, you'll need a 25-foot measuring tape to obtain outside dimensions which you will draw to scale in your deck plans.

Measuring the Site. With your 25-foot measuring tape you can begin to measure the site. Place construction stakes at the perimeter of your imaginary deck. If you are building an attached deck, use the house wall as an initial reference point. Then start to transfer measurements from your deck outline to paper. It is standard practice to orient your base plan drawing with north at the top of the plan. You should include on your base plan all surrounding elements which could influence the final design of your deck—paths or doorways which will provide access to the deck, deck views and privacy considerations, trees and their shadow patterns, other buildings, grade conditions, and any nearby underground utility services.

Finalizing the Design. Once you have transferred your site measurements into the base plan, you can begin to use the base plan to help you create the final drawings for your deck. Carefully study all the elements of the base plan and resolve any final decisions concerning deck size, height, placement, and type of pier construction.

Pier Location Plan. Once you have decided on a final design, you first need to draw a pier location plan which shows the exact placement of the piers in relation to the deck outline and an existing structure if you are building an attached deck. Consult the span charts on pages 15-16 to be certain that your piers are not spaced too far apart for the joist and beam spacing that you have selected.

Deck Framing Plan. Based on the pier location plan, you will draw a deck framing plan that shows exact measurements for the joists and girders on your deck. Some designers find it easier to draw one plan for joist framing and another for girder framing. Remember to consult the table of nominal versus actual dimensions of dimensional lumber (figure 22-B) when you calculate exact lengths of joists and girders. Again consult the span charts on pp. 15-16 to ensure that you have not exceeded maximum design values for joist and girder spans.

Deck Plan. Using your deck framing plan, draw the surface of your deck as it will appear in a bird's eye view from the top. This plan will help you estimate the amount of decking (also see figure 22-A on page 22), railing, and stair material required to complete your deck.

Deck Elevations. You've drawn the layers of your deck construction from the top view when you made the pier location plan, deck framing plan, and deck plan. Using those top-view plans as a guide, you then draw your deck in a sideways view—as deck elevations which show your deck as it will appear from front, back, left, and rear sides.

Drawing a Plan for Your Deck   Continued

LINE #1

EXISTING BUILDING

B

8'-0"

A

90°

10'-0"

6'-0"

LINE #2

C

9'-9 3/4"

12" DIAMETER
CONCRETE PIERS

DECK OUTLINE

1'-0"   7'-0"   7'-0"   1'-0"

PIER LOCATION PLAN

EXISTING BUILDING

1 1/2"

15'-9"

1 1/2"

2"x8" LEDGER

2"x8" @ 24" O.C. FLOOR JOIST

9'-10 1/2"

10'-0"

12'-0"

11'-10 1/2"

11'-9"

1 1/2"

1 1/2"

2'-0"

1 1/2"

2"x8" SKIRT BOARD

2'-0" 2'-0" 2'-0" 2'-0" 2'-0" 2'-0" 2'-0" 2'-0"

12'-0"   4'-0"

CORNER FRAMING
ANCHOR AT EACH
OUTSIDE CORNER

DETAIL "2F"

DECK FRAMING PLAN

EXISTING BUILDING

1'-0" 1 1/4"

4'-2 1/2"

BENCH·A

2"x4" DECK W/ 1/4" SPACING

12'-0"

10'-6 1/4"

4'-2 1/2"

1'-0"

BENCH SUPPORTS

1 1/2"
1 3/4"

BENCH·B

DN 3R

10'-0"

2'-0"

1'-0"   6'-0"   1'-0"

8'-0"   8'-0"   4'-0"

20'-0"

DECK PLAN

Planning the Deck Substructure

Once you have drawn the surface of your deck in a plan view, you must design the deck's supporting substructure. The tables on pp. 15-16 will assist you in planning the critical substructure system of your deck. You should be aware that these tables reflect spans and spacings for a total load of 60 pounds per square foot, which in many localities is the current load requirement for decks mandated by the Uniform Building Code. The total load of 60 p.s.f has two component loads--the first of 10 p.s.f "dead" load plus a second of 50 p.s.f "live" load. While the 60 p.s.f. total load is more than adequate for most substructure designs, special circumstances such as heavy snow loads or the weight of a hot tub will require consultation with a design professional.

Your own local building department may or may not support the 60 p.s.f total load requirement. Again we strongly advise you to consult with your local building department to ensure that your deck substructure will meet local codes.

How to use Deck Spans & Spacings Tables.

Use the tables on pp. 15-16 to plan the substructure of your deck. First determine the species group of the lumber you will use to build the substructure of your deck. If you are planning to use two different lumber species (such as Douglas fir for joists and redwood for posts, beams, and decking), don't forget to use the correct species group in each appropriate chart.

Refer to the illustrated dimensions in figure 14-A below as a graphic guide to the dimensions listed in the tables. For example, Dimension "A" refers to the maximum allowable span for decking boards listed in the Decking Span Table. Dimension "B" measures both joist span and beam spacing which are different names for an identical dimension. Dimension "C" reflects beam spans for a given beam size. Dimension "D" shows the *minimum* post size required to support a given load area (which you calculate by multiplying Dimension "B" by Dimension "C"). Remember that these spans are for solid beams rather than built-up beams. A 4x6 beam (measuring $3\frac{1}{2}$"x$5\frac{1}{2}$") has greater load carrying strength than a beam built from nailing together two 2x6's (measuring 3"x$5\frac{1}{2}$").

Design the Substructure *CAREFULLY.*

In planning the substructure of your deck, remember that you are working with a complex set of variables and that your final design will reflect a choice between competing alternatives. For example, if you increase the number of concrete piers you can reduce joist spans and girder size and spans. However, if your local frost line requires that piers be constructed to a depth of 3 feet, you might want to reduce the number of piers and increase joist and beam spans. Determine a solution which is cost-effective but does not compromise the strength and durability of your deck. A deck which is inadequately supported by its substructure is dangerous and will require costly repairs at a later date.

Decking

Ledger

Joist

Dimension "B"
Joist Span
(same as Beam Spacing)

Post

Dimension "D"
Post Height

Pier Block

Dimension "A"
Decking Span
(same as Joist Spacing)

Dimension "C"
Beam Span
(same as Post Spacing)

DECK SPANS & SPACINGS

CHARTS ARE BASED ON A 60 P.S.F. TOTAL LOAD
50 P.S.F. LIVE LOAD PLUS 10 P.S.F DEAD LOAD

STRENGTH GROUPS OF COMMON SOFTWOODS SPECIES

GROUP I:
DOUGLAS FIR
HEMLOCK, WESTERN
LARCH, WESTERN
PINE, SOUTHERN
SPRUCE

GROUP II:
CEDAR, WESTERN
DOUGLAS FIR (SOUTH)
FIR (WHITE, ALPINE)
HEMLOCK (EASTERN, MOUNTAIN)
PINE (EASTERN WHITE, IDAHO WHITE, LODGEPOLE)
PINE (NORTHERN, PONDEROSA, RED, SUGAR, WESTERN WHITE)
REDWOOD
SPRUCE (EASTERN, ENGELMANN)

DECKING SPAN CHART

Species Group	Maximum Allowable Span — See Dimension "A" on Page 14. Based on 1200 P.S.F. Fibre Strength Lumber--Construction Grade (No. 2) or Better. All spans shown in inches.			
	Laid Flat		**Laid On Edge**	
	1x4, 1x6, $5/4 \times 6$ (S4S,T&G,RadiusEdge)	All 2-by lumber (Standard and T&G)	2x3 lumber (Standard)	2x4 lumber (Standard)
I	16	60	90	144
II	14	48	78	120

JOIST SPAN CHART

Species Group	Joist Size	Maximum Allowable Joist Span — See Dimension "B" on Page 14. Total Load 60 P.S.F.(50 P.S.F. Live Load plus 10 P.S.F. Dead Load) Based on 1200 P.S.F. Fibre Strength Lumber--Construction Grade (No.2) or Better.		
		Maximum Allowable Joist Span		
		Joist Spacing(inches) **16**	**24**	**32**
I	2x6	9'-6"	8'-3"	7'-5"
	2x8	12'-7"	11'-0"	10'-0"
	2x10	16'-1"	14'-0"	12'-10"
II	2x6	8'-4"	7'-4"	6'-6"
	2x8	11'-0"	9'-8"	8'-8"
	2x10	14'-2"	12'-4"	11'-2"

BEAM SPANS AND POST HEIGHTS
CHARTS ARE BASED ON A 60 P.S.F. TOTAL LOAD
50 P.S.F. LIVE LOAD PLUS 10 P.S.F DEAD LOAD

Maximum Allowable Beam Spans
See Dimension "C" on Page 14.
Total Load 60 P.S.F.(50 P.S.F. Live Load plus 10 P.S.F. Dead Load)
Based on 1200 P.S.F. Fibre Strength Lumber--Construction Grade (No.2) or Better.
Beams are on edge. Span distance is center to center between posts or supports.

Species Group	Beam Size	See Dimension "B" Beam Spacing(Feet)								
		4'	5'	6'	7'	8'	9'	10'	11'	12'
I	**4x4**	up to 4'								
	4x6	up to 6'								
	3x8	up to 8'			up to 6'					
	4x8	up to 10'	up to 9'	up to 8'	up to 7'	up to 6'				
	3x10	up to 11'	up to 10'	up to 9'	up to 8'	up to 7'	up to 6'			
	4x10	up to 12'	up to 11'	up to 10'	up to 9'	up to 8'	up to 7'			
	3x12		up to 12'	up to 11'	up to 10'	up to 9'		up to 8'		
	4x12			up to 12'		up to 11'	up to 10'	up to 9'		
	6x10					up to 12'	up to 11'	up to 10'		
	6x12						up to 12'			
II	**4x4**	up to 4'								
	4x6	up to 6'								
	3x8	up to 7'		up to 6'						
	4x8	up to 9'	up to 8'	up to 7'		up to 6'				
	3x10	up to 10'	up to 9'	up to 8'	up to 7'		up to 6'			
	4x10	up to 11'	up to 10'	up to 9'	up to 8'		up to 7'		up to 6'	
	3x12	up to 12'	up to 11'	up to 10'	up to 9'	up to 8'		up to 7'		
	4x12		up to 12'	up to 11'	up to 10'		up to 9'	up to 8'		
	6x10			up to 12'	up to 11'	up to 10'	up to 9'			
	6x12				up to 12'		up to 11'	up to 10'		

Minimum Post Heights (Dimension "D")
(Wood Beam Supports)

Species Group	Post Size(in)	Load Area = Beam spacing(Dimension "B") x Post spacing(Dimension "C") in Square Feet									
		36 LBS.	40 LBS.	60 LBS.	72 LBS.	84 LBS.	96 LBS.	108 LBS.	120 LBS.	132 LBS.	144 LBS.
I	**4x4**	up to 12 ft. heights		up to 10 ft. heights	up to 8 ft. heights						
	4x6					up to 12 ft. heights		up to 10 ft. heights			
	6x6									up to 12 ft. heights	
II	**4x4**	up to 12 ft. heights	up to 10 ft. heights	up to 8 ft. heights							
	4x6			up to 12 ft. heights	up to 10 ft. heights						
	6x6						up to 12 ft. heights				

Planning your Deck Surface

The deck surface is your deck's most visible element and the one that you will have to live with intimately as you use your deck. So careful planning of your deck surface is in order. If cost and ease of construction are your primary considerations, then you should stick with the classic pattern of parallel 2x6's laid perpendicular to the joists. However, if expense is not the primary consideration and you have modest construction experience, you should consider some of the other decking patterns illustrated below.

You should be aware that diagonal decking patterns require closer joist spacing to support longer decking spans when deck boards run diagonal to joists. Consequently, you must plan your deck surface in coordination with planning your deck substructure. As a rule of thumb, a complicated deck surface pattern requires a more complex and costly deck substructure.

A simpler yet visually interesting alternative to diagonal decking is to alternate widths of 2 by dimensional lumber laid flat. See page 18 for patterns you can create by alternating 2x2's, 2x4's, and 2x6's.

You can design a deck surface with 2x3's or 2x4's on edge rather than laid flat. On edge decking is far more expensive than decking laid flat but can span much longer distances between joists.

The modular checkerboard pattern illustrated on page 18 offers bold visual impact and is not as difficult to construct as diagonal decking. However, the squares must be carefully laid out in advance so that support spacings correspond to the dimensions of the square. Extra blocking is often required so that the end of each decking board is directly supported.

Whatever deck pattern you select, space decking boards at least $3/16$" for proper drainage, ventilation, and the natural shrinkage and swelling of wood.

Alternating 2x4's and 2x6's. This pattern provides visual interest while retaining simplicity of construction.

Herringbone 2x6's. More difficult to construct but offers a striking visual effect.

Diagonal 2x6's. Decrease joist spacing to provide additional support for diagonal decking.

Standard parallel 2x6's. This pattern is the easiest to construct of all the decking patterns.

L-Pattern which sets decking perpendicular to joists but requires complex deck substructure.

Checkerboard pattern offers visual impact with relative ease of construction.

2 x 6 and
2 x 4 Wood
Members

Three examples of varying the widths of decking lumber in order to create a dramatic visual effect.

2 x 6 and
2 x 2 Wood
Members

2 x 4 and
2 x 2 Wood
Members

For Notes and Layout Procedures...

For Notes and Layout Procedures...

½"=1'0" Scale

Choosing Lumber for Your Deck

Choosing the correct lumber for your deck can be as consequential as determining the correct design. For use in a deck, the lumber you select must perform well in an exposed outdoor environment. Performance is measured according to the following criteria:

• **Freedom from Shrinkage and Warping.** Lumber which has dimensional stability will not cause problems later. You don't want to have to replace deck boards only 2 or 3 years after construction.

• **Hardness.** Gives your deck durability and prevents marring of the deck surface if sharp objects are dropped.

• **Decay Resistance.** Generally lumber cut from the heartwood (center of the log) is more resistant to decay than lumber cut from sapwood (outside of the log). However, chemical pressure-treatment can provide decay resistance to species which lack this property.

• **Workability.** Refers to the ease with which you can saw, nail, or shape lumber.

• **Nail Holding.** Determines whether or not a given species possesses good nail-holding power.

• **Paint Holding.** The ability to hold a finish. Some species which contain high levels of natural extractives (such as pitch or resins) do not hold a finish well.

• **Fire Resistance.** All woods are combustible, but some resist fire better than others. Woods which do not contain large amounts of resin are relatively slow to ignite.

• **Strength and Weight.** Wood which is relatively light in weight but possesses great strength is ideal.

While no single species performs ideally according to all of the criteria above, your local lumber dealer will be able to advise you regarding the lumber species most suited to your area. Often you must balance considerations of economy with performance. For example, redwood is considered a premium decking material, but high transportation costs outside the area of manufacture make pressure-treated pine woods a more economical alternative.

Here is a concise guide to some common softwood lumber species used in deck construction:

• **Cedar, Western Red.** Popular for the durability and decay-resistance of its heartwood.

• **Cypress.** Cypress resists decay, has an attractive reddish coloration, and holds paint well.

• **Douglas Fir, Larch.** Douglas fir has great strength and is used best in the substructure of your deck, especially in the joist members.

• **Pines.** Numerous pine species have excellent workability but must be pressure-treated for use in deck construction.

• **Southern Pine.** Unlike the soft pines described above, southern pines possess strength but are only moderately decay and warp resistant.

• **Poplar.** Has moderate strength, resists decay and warping.

• **Redwood.** The premium decking material because of its durability, resistance to decay, and beautiful natural brownish-red coloration.

• **Spruce.** Typically spruce species are readily available but do not have great decay resistance.

Remember that in certain circumstances you can use two different species of lumber to construct your deck. For example, redwood can be used for decking and post members while Douglas fir is used for strength in the deck joists and girders.

Whatever lumber species you select, study the illustration below to learn the difference between the grain patterns in dimensional lumber. **Flat grain** lumber is cut with the grain parallel to the face of the board. Typically used for decking, flat grain boards should be used with the bark-side up in order to minimize cupping and grain separation. **Vertical grain** lumber, a more expensive grade used for finish work, is cut with the grain perpendicular to the face of the board.

Lumber Sizes

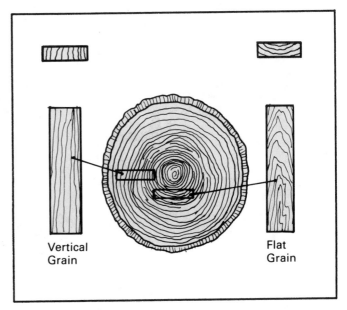

Grain Location

Choosing Lumber for your Deck Continued

The illustration below will give you an idea of some of the defects found in dimensional lumber. Typical defects are **checks** that result from separation of wood across annual rings, **knots** that result from a portion of a tree branch incorporated in cust lumber, and **splits** which are a separation of the wood due to tearing apart of wood cells. A **shake** is a lengthwise separation of the wood which usually occurs between the rings of annual growth. None of the above defects should cause you to reject lumber outright. However, wood with a **bow, cup, crook, wane, split** or **twist** should be avoided in deck construction.

Dimensional lumber is typically sold in incremental lengths of 2 feet--for example, 2x6 decking comes in lengths of 8,10,12,14,16,and 20 feet. When you plan your deck, you should try to consider standard board lengths in the overall dimensions of your deck. A 12'x16' deck (192 sq. ft.) will be far more economical to build than a deck measuring 11' x 18' (198 sq. ft.) due to wastage.

The chart below shows you how many decking boards to purchase for a given deck width in feet. If your deck is greater than 16 or 20 feet in length, however, you will need to purchase at least two different board lengths for every run of decking.

Remember that the nominal dimensions of lumber do not indicate the actual finished size of dimensional lumber. For example, a 2x6 decking board measures approximately 1½" x 5½" depending upon moisture content and surface. Lumber that has a **rough** surface will measure close to the nominal size in comparison to lumber that is surfaced on four sides (known as **S4S**).

The most critical factor in determining actual sizes of dimensional lumber is the moisture content of the wood. Look for the grade stamp imprinted on lumber to determine moisture content. Typical moisture content ratings are:

- **MC 15** (less than 15% moisture content)
- **S-DRY** (less than 19% moisture content)
- **S-GRN** (greater than 19% moisture content)

A 2x6 surfaced unseasoned board (S-GRN) will actually measure $1\,^9/_{16}$" x $5\,^5/_8$" compared to $1\,^1/_2$" x $5\,^1/_2$" for a 2x6 rated surfaced dry (S-DRY). The chart below shows actual versus nominal sizes of dimensional lumber which is S4S and S-DRY or better.

It is wise to avoid unseasoned lumber especially in the selection of your decking. Decking which is unseasoned can shrink considerably as it dries naturally and will leave hazardous gaps over ¼" between deck boards.

DECK BOARDS REQUIRED FOR A GIVEN DECK WIDTH IN FEET
ASSUMES ³/₁₆" SPACING BETWEEN DECK BOARDS

Deck Width:	8	9	10	11	12	13	14	15	16	17	18	19	20	21	22	23	24
2x4's Laid Flat	26	29	33	36	39	42	46	49	52	56	59	62	66	69	72	75	79
2x6's Laid Flat	16	18	21	23	25	27	29	31	33	35	37	39	42	44	46	48	50
2-by's On Edge	56	63	71	78	85	92	99	106	113	120	127	134	142	149	156	163	170

Figure 22-A

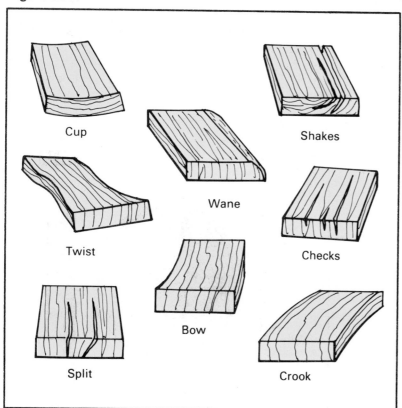

Cup

Shakes

Wane

Twist

Checks

Split

Bow

Crook

STANDARD DIMENSIONS OF SURFACED LUMBER

Nominal size	Surfaced (actual) size
1 × 2	3/4" × 1-1/2"
1 × 3	3/4" × 2-1/2"
1 × 4	3/4" × 3-1/2"
1 × 6	3/4" × 5-1/2"
1 × 8	3/4" × 7-1/4"
1 × 10	3/4" × 9-1/4"
1 × 12	3/4" × 11-1/4"
2 × 3	1-1/2" × 2-1/2"
2 × 4	1-1/2" × 3-1/2"
2 × 6	1-1/2" × 5-1/2"
2 × 8	1-1/2" × 7-1/4"
2 × 10	1-1/2" × 9-1/4"
2 × 12	1-1/2" × 11-1/4"
4 × 4	3-1/2" × 3-1/2"
4 × 10	3-1/2" × 9-1/4"
6 × 8	5-1/2" × 7-1/2"

Figure 22-B

Ordering Deck Materials

Complete the sample material list below before you begin to shop. If you are using one of the deck plans offered in the back of this manual, each plan comes with a complete bill of materials. If you have designed your own deck, create a material list from the final design after approval by your local building department.

Once you have completed the sample material list, you should visit several reputable building supply dealers to shop for your materials. Be aware that you will add to the cost of your project if you purchase your materials in a piecemeal fashion. Obtain competitive bids on your bill of materials from different dealers. Keep in mind that the quality of materials and the level of service provided by the dealer are hidden factors in selecting your supplier. Some dealers will offer you a low price but will not provide free on-site delivery. Delivery charges can more than offset a low initial bid.

Especially consider the quality and grade of the lumber you are purchasing. Poor quality materials will yield a meager return on your deck investment. Finally, if you are a novice Do-It-Yourselfer, don't forget that a dealer who provides knowledgeable service as well as economical materials can save you from costly and time-consuming errors.

Don't hesitate to order at least a 5-10% overage of materials to make up for inevitable cutting mistakes or lumber defects. Be aware that dimensional lumber is sold either by the board foot, the lineal (or running) foot, or by the piece. A board foot of lumber represents the amount of lumber in a board 1" thick x 12" wide x 12" long. Use the following formula to compute board feet:

$$\text{Board Feet} = \frac{\text{Length(Feet) x Width(Inches) x Thickness(Inches)}}{12}$$

Sample Materials List

	SIZE	LENGTH	QUANTITY	X	COST	=	TOTAL COST
FOUNDATION							
Concrete							
Sand							
Gravel							
SUBSTRUCTURE							
Posts							
Girders							
Deck Joists							
Rim Joists							
Ledger							
Bracing							
Fascia / Trim Boards							
Miscellaneous							
SURFACE LUMBER							
Decking							
STAIRS							
Stair Stringer							
Stair Riser							
Stair Tread							
RAILINGS							
Railings							
Balusters							
CONNECTORS							
Nails							
Joist Hangers							
Joist Anchors							
Post Base Anchors							
Post Caps							
Lag Bolts w/ Washers							
Screws							
GRAND TOTAL							

Nails and Fasteners for Deck Construction

Nails are the most common fastener used in deck framing and construction. Nail lengths are indicated by the term penny, noted by a small letter **d.** In most cases, nails increase in diameter as they increase in length. Heavier construction framing is accomplished with common nails. The extra thick shank of the common nail has greater strength than other types. A wide thick head spreads the load and resists pull-through. For the substructure of your deck where nails are hidden, consider vinyl coated sinkers or cement coated nails which bond to the wood and will not pull up as readily as uncoated nails.

To fasten your decking planks to deck joists, use **hot-dipped galvanized** common nails, typically 10d. or longer. To prevent splitting, predrill nail holes through decking. Spiral nails or annular ring nails provide greater holding power and are less likely to pull up with weathering of your deck. If you have selected redwood for decking, avoid poor-quality nails which will react with the decay-resisting substances in the wood and cause unsightly stains. Finally, consider **deck screws** as the most expensive but most flexible means of fastening your decking. Deck screws will not pull out and easily allow replacement of individual deck boards at a later time.

Box nails are similar in shape to common nails, but they have a slimmer shank that is less likely to split wood. Finishing nails are used in work where you want to counter sink and then cover the nail head.

Screws create neat, strong joints for finished work. Heavy-duty **lag screws** and **lag bolts** are useful for heavier framing connections, such as girder-to-post.

Discuss your project with your local hardware or building supply dealer to determine the best nail and fastener selections for your deck project.

FINISHING NAIL SELECTION CHART

SIZE	LENGTH	GAUGE	APP. # PER LB.
10d	3"	11½	120
8d	2½"	12½	190
6d	2"	13	310
4d	1½"	15	600
3d	1¼"	15½	870
2d	1"	16	1000

TABLE OF COMMON NAILS

SIZE	LENGTH	GAUGE	#PER LB.
2d	1"	15	840
3d	1¼"	14	540
4d	1½"	12½	290
5d	1¾"	12½	250
6d	1"	11½	160
7d	2¼"	11½	150
8d	2½"	10¼	100
9d	2¾"	10¼	90
10d	3"	9	65
12d	3¼"	9	60
16d	3½"	8	45
20d	4"	6	30
30d	4½"	5	20
40d	5"	4	16
50d	5½"	3	12
60d	6"	2	10

This table of common nails shows the approximate number of nails you get in a pound. You'll need more pounds of larger sizes to do a job. For outside jobs, get galvanized or cadmium-plated nails. Aluminum nails are a bit expensive unless you're doing a small project.

Common Nail · Box Nail · Finishing Nail · Casing Nail · Vinyl-Coated Sinker · Deck Screw · Lag Screw · Machine Bolt · Carriage Bolt · Spiral Nail · Annular Ring Nail · Metal Anchor · Washer · Nut

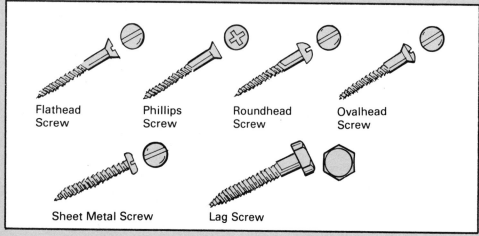

Flathead Screw · Phillips Screw · Roundhead Screw · Ovalhead Screw · Sheet Metal Screw · Lag Screw

SCREW SELECTION CHART

Size	Length	Size	Length
0	1/4-3/8	9	1/2-3
1	1/4-1/2	10	1/2-31/2
2	1/4-3/4	11	5/8-31/2
3	1/4-1	12	5/8-4
4	1/4-11/2	14	3/4-5
5	3/8-11/2	16	1-5
6	3/8-21/2	18	11/4-5
7	3/8-21/2	20	11/2-5
8	3/8-3	24	3-5

This chart shows sizes and the lengths in which they're available. The larger sizes come in longer lengths. Most jobs call for sizes 6 to 12 in ½ to 3 inch lengths. Check size and length before you buy.

Framing with Metal Fasteners

A wide variety of metal fasteners are available to make your deck sturdy and long-lasting. You may be required by local codes to add **seismic/hurricane connectors** to each joist where it connects to the supporting girder. **Post cap connectors** and the **anchor base connectors** illustrated below are a superior means of fastening compared to toenailing. Be certain that connectors are level and square before you secure the post with nails at the nailing holes in the metal connector. Follow the manufacturer's installation instructions.

Right-angled **corner framing anchors** add strength to perpendicular butt joints, especially where rim joists meet. Use **joist hangers** to attach your deck joists to rim joist members. The modest additional expense of metal fasteners will be more than offset by the added durability of your deck. Remember that metal fasteners help your deck to withstand the expansion and contraction of wood that occurs with changes of season. Secure fasteners using the short ribbed nails provided or where extra strength is required use lag screws in addition to nails.

Courtesy of Simpson Strong-Tie Co. Inc.

Post Base Anchor

Available sizes for:
4 x 4 Posts
4 x 6 Posts
6 x 6 Posts

Post Anchor

Available sizes for:
4x and 6x Posts

Adjustable Post Anchor

Available sizes for:
4 x 4 Posts
4 x 6 Posts
6 x 6 Posts

Framing with Metal Fasteners Continued

Post Base

Available sizes for:
4 x 4 Posts
4 x 6 Posts
6 x 6 Posts

Joist Hangers

Available sizes for:
2 x 4 Joists
2 x 6 Joists
2 x 8 Joists
2 x 10 Joists
2 x 12 Joists

Beam Frame Connector

Available sizes for:
2 x 4 Joists
2 x 6 Joists

Courtesy of Simpson Strong-Tie Co., Inc.

BUILDING YOUR DECK

**GENERIC STEP-BY-STEP INSTRUCTIONS
FOR BUILDING A LOW-LEVEL ATTACHED DECK**

1.Site Preparation:

• Obtain a building permit if required and ensure that you will not be building your deck on top of sewer, gas, or electrical lines that require service. Grade your site and install drainage if necessary.

2.Laying Out the Deck:

• Mark the position of the deck on your house wall following the deck framing plan. Measure out from the house the depth of your deck and drive a stake to mark each corner. Construct batter boards two feet each way past the outer corners using 2x4 stakes. The top of the batter boards must be level. Extend string lines across the batter boards to outline the deck. Place additional stakes for string lines to locate the top of concrete piers. Each string line should be taut and level. Your outline can also be squared by measuring along one side a distance of 4 feet and along the adjacent side a distance of 3 feet. Your outline will be square when the diagonal dimension between the two points measures 5 feet. Repeat the process at the opposite corner.

3. Locating Deck Piers:

• Following the deck framing plan, locate the piers. Place a wood stake in the ground to mark the center of each pier. The string lines you placed above will help you to determine the correct top height for each pier.

4. Determining Height of Deck:

• In order to determine the height of your deck you must first determine the height of your house floor from your grade line. Once you have determined this height, allow for a 2" to 4" step down from your house floor to the deck so that water will not enter the house. The remaining dimension will be the height of your post from the bottom of the girder to grade line.

5. Attaching the Ledger:

• Cut ledger to size and brace against the house wall at desired height. Level the ledger with carpenter's level. Temporarily nail the ledger in place at opposite ends and then recheck for level. Once ledger is level, secure to house with $3/8$" lag screws that are at least 2" longer than the thickness of the ledger. Use a washer on each fastener and space at 24" maximum intervals.

6. Installing Piers and Posts:

• Dig pier holes 12" in diameter to the necessary depth required by your area. The depth of the hole should be at least half the height of the 4x4 post above ground. Some local codes require that your pier hole extend at least 6 inches below the local frost line.

Piers and Posts (continued):

• If you are using precast concrete piers, fill the hole with sufficient concrete to embed the pier at least 4" in the concrete and set the pier square and level in its footing. Use the string line to adjust the pier to the correct height. Fasten post base anchor to nailer block on pier.

• If you are creating your own pier, build pier forms then fill the hole with concrete. When concrete first starts to set, position a post base anchor in each pier and make sure the post base is centered and level.

• Begin to secure 4x4 posts by starting with the lower level post closest to the house. This post will serve as the base post for setting the heights of all other posts. Tie a string line to a nail set flush with the top of the ledger board. Extend the other end of the string over the top of the base post and attach a line level and mark each post at proper height. Cut off excess post. Plumb and square post with a level. Nail posts to post base anchors.

7. Installing the Girders:

• Cut the girders to their proper lengths following the deck framing plan. Square up corners of girders and be sure all outer edges are in line. Secure girders to posts with post cap connectors.

8. Attaching Joists and Rim Joists:

• Cut the rim joists to their proper lengths. Attach metal joist hangers to ledger board at 16" or 24" intervals and to opposite rim joist at proper interval. Make certain hangers are square and at proper height.

• Set the first joist in first hanger on the ledger board. This joist should be level on the top of the girders if you have planned correctly. Install remaining joists in their hangers. Set the rim joist opposite the ledger in place and secure by fastening joists to joist hangers.

• Secure two additional rim joists to ledger board and opposite rim joist with corner framing anchors.

• Ensure that all rim joists are square and that deck joists are straight in hangers. Nail deck joists to hangers and use joist ties to fasten joists to girders.

9. Nailing the Decking:

• Start with the first board along the house wall and allow a $3/8$" expansion joint between first board and the wall. Since this first board will serve as a guide for the rest of the decking, place it as square as possible. To prevent against splitting, pre-drill slightly undersized pilot holes at each location where your will fasten decking to the joist. Use three 12 penny hot-dipped galvanized nails at the end of each board and two nails at the joists. Snap a chalk line to keep your nails in a straight line. Use 16 penny nails as spacers for a $3/16$" gap between deck boards. When 6 feet of decking remains to be placed, adjust board spacing to avoid a gap at the end of the deck.

• When all the decking is in place, snap a chalk line along the outside face of the end joists. Cut the deck boards at the chalk line so they're flush with rim joists. Set trim boards flush with decking top and nail to rim joists.

10. Finishing:

• If you so desire, apply a paint or stain to your finished deck in accordance with the manufacturer's instructions provided with the product.

Laying out the Deck and Locating Piers

• Check and recheck your foundation pier layout plan. Errors at this stage are costly and difficult to correct. You must layout the deck and locate piers with accuracy.

• Be certain that you know the location of all underground utility and septic lines that may interfere with construction of your deck. Do **NOT** locate your deck over or near an active septic tank.

• Mark the position of your ledger board on your house wall following the deck framing plan. You can either install the ledger (see pages 30-31) temporarily at this time or pencil mark the location and install the ledger later.

• Measure out from the house the depth of your deck and drive a stake to mark each corner. Construct **batter boards** 24" each way past the outer corners using 2x4 stakes as shown below. Drive the stakes holding the batter boards securely into the ground. Use your carpenter's level and a straight 2x4 or a string level on a nylon string to ensure that the tops of the batter boards are level and at the same height as the top of your ledger.

• Extend nylon string lines across the batter boards to outline the deck. Each **perimeter string** should be taut and level. It helps to cut a notch at the top of the batter board to hold the string line securely in place.

• To ensure squareness form a **3-4-5 right triangle** with the string lines. Using a felt tipped pen, mark the string line 4 feet out from where the lines intersect. Then mark the other line 3 feet out from the crossing point. Finally measure the distance diagonally between the marks on both string lines. When the distance measures exactly five feet your deck outline is square. Remember that the system of the 3-4-5 right triangle works in any multiple of 3-4-5 such as 6-8-10 or 9-12-15. Repeat this process at each corner of the deck.

• Check that your work is square by measuring diagonally from opposite corner marks in an **X** formation. If your diagonal measurements are equal, your deck perimeter layout is aligned properly. If the measurements are not equal, recheck your work and adjust string lines until they are correct.

• Next determine the location for each pier following the deck foundation pier layout plan. Measure along opposite perimeter strings and mark the points that represent the pier centerline(s). Place a stake at these marks and then attach a level string to show the centerline of the piers. This string should be at the same height as the perimeter strings. Mark the location of each pier on the **pier centerline string** and drop a plumb bob to mark the center of each pier. Identify the center of each pier location with a stake. Place a string for each row of piers.

Digging Pier Holes

• Dig pier holes 10"-12" in diameter. It's best to move the string lines temporarily before you dig. Depth of pier holes depends upon your local building codes and the level of your local frost line. Use a shovel or post hole digger to dig holes with straight rather than sloping sides. Dig the hole deep enough to allow for 4" of compacted gravel at the bottom of the hole.

• Tamp the soil at the bottom of the hole to prevent settling of the pier. Add approximately 4" of gravel to the bottom of the hole. At this point you can add reinforcing bar if your local codes require it. The reinforcing bar adds strength to deep concrete piers. The completed hole should be deep enough to allow the top of the completed pier to sit approximately 4"-6" inches above the finished grade line. Replace string lines and recheck your work.

Attaching The Ledger Board to Your Home

• Study the illustrations below and on page 31 which demonstrate different methods of attaching a ledger board to the outside wall of your home.

• Select only a straight board which is either pressure-treated or cut from a decay resistant species such as redwood or cedar for your ledger. You don't want the ledger to warp or decay and cause sévere problems at a later date.

• Position the ledger so that you step down from the house onto the deck. If the ledger board is higher than your house floor, water can run into the house from the deck. Remember that you will apply decking on top of the ledger and joist subsystem when you determine the height of the ledger in relation to the house floor.

• Be sure to locate and reroute if necessary all utility lines which might run in the wall where you will attach the ledger.

• Brace the ledger against the house wall at the desired height.

• Mark holes for lag bolts or screws on the ledger board. Typically the holes occur in pairs, one on top of the other, at the end of the ledger and then alternate in an up and down pattern. See figure 31-A on page 31. Be careful not to place your holes where you will affix joist hangers.

• Use rustproof hot-dipped galvanized lag screws or bolts. If you are fastening the ledger to aluminum siding, use aluminum screws and washers to prevent corrosion.

• For **wooden walls**, temporarily nail once at the board's approximate center, level the board with a carpenter's level, and temporarily nail both ends. Recheck for levelness. If the ledger is level, fasten to the wall with lag screws and washers. To prevent trapping of moisture between the ledger and the exterior wall, you might want to place two or three washers over the lag screw on the back (house) side of the ledger to act as spacers.

• For **stucco walls**, first drill lag screw holes into the ledger with a wood bit. Then use makeshift braces for support or enlist extra helping hands to hold the ledger in position and mark the stucco through the ledger holes with a pencil. Be certain that the ledger is level before you mark the holes on the stucco. These marked holes must be drilled with a masonry bit in order to penetrate the stucco. Once you have drilled through the stucco, you can again switch to a wood bit and then drill a slightly undersized hole (for example use a $1/4$" bit for $3/8$" lag screws) into the house floor frame header board.

• For **masonry walls**, drill lag screw holes into the ledger with a wood bit. Then use makeshift braces for support or enlist extra helping hands to hold the ledger in position and mark the masonry through the ledger holes with a pencil. Be certain that the ledger is level before you mark the holes on the masonry. Drill with a masonry bit and create a hole wide and deep enough to accommodate an expansion shield for the lag bolt. Carefully seat the expansion shield, place the ledger board against the wall, and secure with lag bolts and washers.

• You might want to paint the exposed cut ends of the ledger with a preservative to prevent decay.

Attaching to Masonry

Attaching to Wood

Bolting Ledger to House

Siding

Flooring

Box Sill

Foundation Wall

2" to 4"

Level

Ledger

Brace

Grade

4"

Single Bolting 16" to 24" O.C.

2"

16" to 24"
O. C.

2 1/2"

Ledger Board

Figure 31-A   31

Installing Piers and Posts

• First be certain you have purchased enough concrete to complete pier installation. Concrete is measured in cubic yards. To calculate the concrete required for a given number of cylindrical piers, use the following formula to find the **Total Volume in cubic yards:**

$$\text{Volume} = \frac{3.14 \times \text{Depth of Pier(Feet)} \times \text{Diameter (Feet)} \times \text{Diameter(Feet)} \times \text{No. Piers}}{108}$$

Example: Concrete required for twelve 10" diameter piers, 30" deep.

$$\text{Volume in cubic yards} = \frac{3.14 \times 2.5 \times .83 \times .83 \times 12}{108} = 0.61 \text{ Cubic Yards}$$

Remember to <u>convert</u> inches to feet (10 inches = .83 feet)
Conversion Factor: 27 Cubic Feet=1 Cubic Yard

• Prepare pier forms if you are going to make poured in-place piers. Otherwise obtain precast piers with a redwood or pressure-treated nailer block on top. You might want to temporarily remove pier centerline strings at this point.

• Mix concrete according to manufacturer's instructions in a wheelbarrow or in a "half-bag" mixer. Use clean water for mixing and achieve the proper plastic consistency before you pour the concrete. If you are not using ready-mix concrete, prepare a **1:2:3 mix**—one part concrete, two parts river sand, and three parts gravel.

• Coat the inside of the forms with oil to prevent sticking and dampen the inside of the hole with water before you pour the concrete.

• With your post base anchors at hand, pour the concrete into the forms and tamp slightly to settle. For **poured in-place piers**, wait for the concrete to begin to harden and set the post base anchors into the concrete. Ensure that anchors are square and level. You can drop a plumb bob from your centerline string to be certain that your anchor is centered properly. Adjust post base anchors to the correct height.

• If you are using a **precast pier**, fill the pier hole with concrete up to 2"-3" below grade level. Then spray the pier with water and then embed the pier at least 3" into the fresh concrete and twist slightly to achieve a solid bond between the concrete and the pier. Make certain that you have enough concrete in the hole so that the top of the nailer block is at least 4"-6" above grade level. Check the alignment of the pier by dropping the plumb bob from the centerline string. Finally, use a level across the nailer block and tap the pier until it is level in all directions and square.

• Allow the concrete to harden at least 24 hours before you proceed to attach posts to piers. If you have poured your concrete during hot and dry conditions, you should cover the piers with wet burlap sacks to encourage a slow cure of the concrete.

• If you are using precast piers and decide to secure post anchor connectors to the nailer block, wait for concrete to harden and then nail the post anchors to the nailer block with short ribbed nails.

Post Hole Digger

Pre-Made 12" Dia. Fiberboard Tube

Nail Into Form Work

2 x 4 Bracing

Post Base Anchor

12" Diameter Concrete Pier

Installing Piers and Posts   Continued

Tapered
Pier Form

Metal Connector   Nailing Block

6" x 6" x 12"
Form For Pier

Alternate Installation and Base Anchor Techniques

**Post Base
Anchor**

**Elevated
Post Base**

**Post Base
Anchor**

**Adjustable
Post Base
Anchor**

**Post
Base
Anchor**

Courtesy of Simpson Strong-Tie Co., Inc.

Measuring Deck Post Height

• If you are building railings, some posts will extend above the deck floor to provide railing support. Follow the post bracing instructions for high-level decks but do not cut posts at the girder line.

• Cut deck posts individually to at least 6" longer than finished post height. If you are uncertain as to the approximate finished height, drop your plumb bob from the pier centerline string and measure the distance from the string (which should be at the height of the *top* of the girder) to the bottom seat of post anchor connector or to the top of the nailing block. First *subtract* the actual height (remember that a 4x6 girder for example is only 5 1/2" high) of the girder and then add 6" to this distance to calculate your rough-in post height.

• If your deck is a **low-level deck** with short posts (under 12"), simply seat the rough-in posts in the post anchor connectors, check for plumb with a level, and ensure that posts are square in the connector. Use either the pier centerline string to establish a cutting line on the post or use a string level on a line from the top of the ledger board to the post. Again you must *subtract* the actual (versus nominal) height of the girder from your string line to establish the **cutting line** on the post.

• If your deck is a **high-level deck** with posts over 12", use the following instructions to ensure that posts are plumb and cut at the correct height for the girder.

• Follow the illustration below and use scrap lumber to stake and support the post. First use a carpenter's level on two adjacent sides of the post to ensure that the post is plumb and then use a string level to determine the correct height of the post in relation to the ledger board. Remember that you must subtract the actual height of the girder from your stringline to establish your cutting line. Mark the cutting line with a pencil.

• Cut marked posts at the post cutting line. Be certain that your cut through the post is a level cut.

• Recheck your posts for plumb and either **toenail** (driving the nails at an angle on all four sides) the post to the pier's nailing block or seat the post in the **post anchor** and use short ribbed nails provided with the connector or at least 10 penny common HDG nails to connect the post to the post anchor. Nail at all the nailing holes provided in the post anchor. In earthquake prone regions, you can use lag screws to connect the post and the anchor for extra security.

Setting and Plumbing Posts

4" x 4" Post

Use a Level to Plumb Each Post into Position

2" x 4" Stake and Brace

Level

Concrete Pier

Subtract Actual Thickness of Girder

Cutting Line

String level

Ledger

Wall

Brace

Post

Grade

Pre-Made Concrete Pier and Footing

Installing the Girders

• Girders can be either solid or built-up from two or more 2-by boards on edge. Remember that because of extra thickness 4-by beams will support a greater load than built-up 2-by beams. Also a 4x6 girder for example sits squarely on top of a 4x4 post (both are 3 1/2" wide) while two 2x6's spliced together (2 x 1 1/2"=3") do not make an even connection. Whatever type of girder you select, make certain that girders are true and not badly bowed.

• You might need some extra hands to lift a heavy girder into place. Use shims between girder and posts where necessary to correct for short post height and level girder before fastening to post. For the best joining of girder to post, use **post cap connectors** (see illustrations below for various girder to post connector options). Otherwise you can toenail girders to posts with 16 or 20 penny HDG common nails.

Girder Connectors

Post Base Connector

Beam Base Connector

Beam Base Connector

Deck Joist Tie Connector

Beam Leveler Connector

Post Cap Connector

Post Cap Connector

Courtesy of Simpson Strong-Tie Co., Inc.

Attaching Joists and Rim Joists

• First place rim joists (also known as perimeter or band joists) on edge at ends of ledger. Locate the joists so that the bow side of the board is facing up. Next attach rim joist to ledger with **corner framing anchors** or toenail to ledger board with 12 penny common nails. Be certain that rim joists run at a true right angle to your ledger.

• Place the rim joist opposite the ledger board and use corner anchors and nails to secure the connection. Make sure that all rim joists and ledger meet at right angles and realign them if they do not.

• Depending on the joist spacing indicated on your deck framing plan, mark the center location of **joist hangers** on both the ledger and the opposite rim joist. Affix joist hangers with short ribbed nails provided in accordance with the manufacturer's instructions.

• Measure each joist individually and cut to size. Set the first joist in its hangers on the ledger board and opposite rim joist. This joist should be level on the top of the girders if you have planned correctly. Making sure that the joist is level and perpendicular, nail to both joist hangers. Follow this procedure until all joists are installed.

• If you are using 2x8 or larger joists, you should consider installing cross blocking boards or metal cross bracing at mid-span to keep joists from flexing over spans greater than 8 feet.

• Use **seismic/hurricane connectors** (also known as **joist anchors**) illustrated at the bottom of page 37 to secure each joist as it crosses a girder. Otherwise toenail joist to beam with common nails on both sides of the joist.

Basic Deck Components

Attaching Joists and Rim Joists Continued

Joist Hanger

Beam Frame Connector

Seismic/Hurricane Anchor

Twist Strap Metal Connectors

Courtesy of Simpson Strong-Tie Co., Inc.

Bracing Suggestions for High Deck Construction

• Consult your local building codes for post bracing requirements for high decks. Additional factors which require post bracing are high winds, unusual deck loads like a portable spa placed on the deck surface, or earthquake activity.

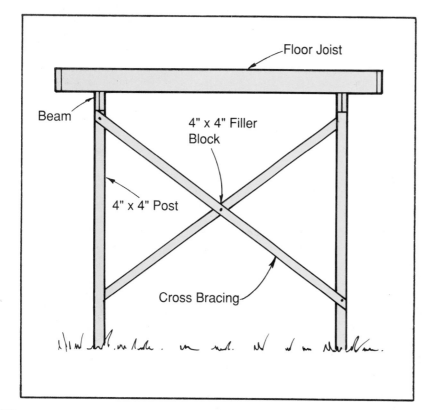

• Use 2x4's to brace distances less than 8 feet and 2x6's for distances greater than 8 feet.

• Use at least four $3/8$" x 3" lag screws and washers (two at each connection point) when you attach the brace to the post.

• If you are using the **X-brace** shown at the left, drill a hole where the braces intersect and secure the braces with one $3/8$" x $3\,1/2$" lag bolt and washer.

• If you construct the **Y-brace** shown at upper left, leave approximately $1/4$" gap between the two braces where they come together to ensure proper drainage. The angle where your braces meet on the post should not exceed 90 degrees.

• Always cut your braces on the diagonal and cover the entire width of the post to which the brace is connected. Square cut braces detract from the appearance of your deck.

Stair Construction

• A solid concrete stair pad is the key to successful stair construction. Don't attempt to anchor your stairs directly into the ground. Add stairs before you place surface decking.

• When you have more than three steps up to your deck, you should construct a hand rail on each side of the stairs. Consult your local building code requirements.

• Two stair construction methods are illustrated below—using **cut stringers** (upper) or the **stair support method** (lower). Instructions for cutting stringers are provided on page 40. The following instructions utilize the stair support method which is easier for the novice builder.

• Measure the vertical height (rise) from grade to top of decking. For a 7" stair rise, divide rise dimension by 7" which will tell you how many stair risers are required. You will need two 10-1/4" **metal stair supports** for each stair and two 2x6 stair treads cut to a minimum 36" stair width.

• Cut 2x10 or 2x12 stair stringers to size and fasten to the deck framing with a 3" corner angles and 1/4" x 1 1/2" lag screws. Use a masonry bit to drill holes for expansion shields into stair pad. Use lag screws to connect bottom corner angles to stringers and measure stringers to ensure they are parallel at top and bottom. Bolt bottom corner angles to expansion shields. Mark the step support positions on both stringers with the support below the stair tread. Use 1/4" x 1 1/2" lag screws to fasten 10-1/4" step supports to stringers and to install 2x6 stair treads.

2" x 12" Cutout Stringer

3" Corner Angle

2" x 12" Stringer with Staircase Angles

Staircase Angle

5'   4'   3'   2'   1'

7" Riser
12" Tread

6 1/2" Riser
13" Tread

6" Riser
14" Tread

5 1/2" Riser
15" Tread

5" Riser
16" Tread

4 1/2" Riser
17" Tread

39

Cutting Stair Stringers

• If you decide to attempt to cut your own stair stringers rather than use metal stair supports, you must select solid 2x12 material free from knots and other defects for your stringers.

• A stair stringer cutting template is available to help you cut stringers. See page 55 for template information.

STRINGER INSTRUCTIONS:
(See illustration at top of page 41)

1. Measure the distance from the top of the deck to the grade in inches. Divide distance by 7.25". round off the solution to the next higher whole number. Divide the distance from the top of the porch to the grade by this whole number. The solution to the step you just completed will be your riser height.

Example:

Top of Porch to Grade=24"

$$\frac{24"}{7.25"} = 3.3"$$

Round off 3.3 to 3. This represents the number of risers.
Divide top of deck to grade distance by the number of risers.

$$\frac{24"}{3} = 8"$$

Round off decimal amount if any to the nearest fractional value in sixteenths of an inch. This example will have 3 risers at 8" each. The size of the tread will be 10 $\frac{3}{4}$" wide. This will allow room for the edge of a riser and two 2x6 treads with a $\frac{1}{4}$" gap between each tread.

---

2. Place a carpenter's square on a 2x12 as shown on page 41. Locate the 10 $\frac{3}{4}$" mark on the outside of the square's long leg. Place this mark on an edge of the 2x12. While holding this point in place, rotate the square until you can read your riser dimension on the outside edge of the short leg. Line the riser dimension up with the edge of the 2x12. Draw a line along both outside edges of the square. This marking constitutes one square and riser.

3. Slide the square along the 2x12 until you can align the 10 $\frac{3}{4}$" mark with the intersections of the edge of the board and the top of the first riser you marked. Again while holding this point in place, rotate the square until you can read your riser dimension on the outside edge of the short leg. Line the riser dimension up with the edge of the 2x12. Draw lines along both outside edges of the square. This mark outlines the second tread and riser.

3. (Continued). Repeat this process until you have drawn the required number of risers for your site condition.

4. Once all the treads and risers have been marked, move down to the line at the base of the first riser and extend that line across the 2x12. Measure 3 $\frac{1}{2}$" up from this line and draw a parallel line. This line is the actual bottom of the stringer.

Note: *This 3 -1/2" is a constant regardless of what you have calculated your particular riser height to be. The 3 -1/2" is made up from the 1 -1/2" thickness of the first tread and the 2" thickness of the concrete that is above grade.*

5. Next extend the line formed by the top tread. Measure along this line 3 $\frac{1}{2}$" past the line of the top riser to locate the back of the stringer. Draw a line from this point, perpendicular to the tread, and extend to underside of stringer.

6. To lay out the notch in the underside of the stringer extend the line of the top riser to the underside of the stringer. Measure over 1 $\frac{1}{2}$" and draw a parallel line. Now take the carpenter's square and place the 1 $\frac{1}{2}$" mark from the outside edge of the square's long leg on the point where the line of the top riser intersects the underside of the stringer. Rotate the long leg of the square until it is parallel with the treads. When it is parallel, the short leg of the square will fall along the line measured 1 $\frac{1}{2}$" over from the line of the top riser. Connect the two lines with a perpendicular line drawn along the outside edge of the square's long leg.

7. Cut out the stringer on the lines that form the treads and risers, the bottom of the stringer, the back of the stringer, and the notch in the underside. Use your power saw carefully and cut each line exactly. Check the stringer by putting it in place on the rim joist and concrete pad. When one stringer has been cut correctly, you can use it as a template for the other two stringers. Again be certain that you do not cut stringers beyond the marked lines.

8. Measure for proper width between stringers at deck attachment point and attach stringers to the deck by using either a corner anchor or joist hanger. Then measure stringers at pad for proper width and mark holes for expansion shields in concrete. Drill holes with a masonry bit. Affix 5" corner anchor to concrete pad and to stringers using $\frac{1}{4}$" x 1 $\frac{1}{2}$" lag screws and washers. Nail each stair tread with bark side up to the stringer with 12 penny hot-dipped galvanized nails or use at least 3" deck screws. You might want to predrill nail holes to prevent splitting of the stair treads.

Two Stair Support Methods:

10 ³/₄" **10 ³/₄"** **8"** **8"** **Varies!** **11 ¹/₄"**

2" x 6" Treads and Risers

Joist Hanger

2" x 12" Stringer

Concrete Slab

Steps with Notched Stringers

Varies

11 ¹/₄"

Varies

Metal Hanger

Staircase Angles

2" x 8" Stringer

Concrete Slab

Staircase Angle

Steps with Staircase Angles Holding Treads

Laying Decking

• Installing decking boards provides great satisfaction as your deck nears completion. However, since the decking is the most visible part of your deck, you must proceed carefully as you nail the decking in place.

• Select decking boards that are straight and free from defects. If you try to use severely warped or bowed lumber, your installation process will be tedious and you will be unhappy with the finished result.

• The following instructions are for parallel decking boards laid flat and installed perpendicular to deck joists. If you are installing your decking on the diagonal, these exact instructions do not apply but the methods are similar. For diagonal decking you still start from one edge and work out from that edge until all decking is in place.

• Select the straightest piece of decking for the first board and place this board at the ledger side of your deck. Place all decking boards bark or convex side up to minimize cupping and checking (see figure 43-A). The first board should be placed $3/8$" from the house wall to allow for drainage.

• Be sure to use only **hot-dipped galvanized nails (HDG)** to fasten decking.

• If your budget allows, you can also consider **ring-shanked nails** or **spiral nails** which are specifically designed for extra holding power. You might not want any deck nails to show—in that case investigate **deck board ties** which cannot be seen (see illustration on page 43) Finally, you can also use 3" or longer **deck screws**.

• Typically you will use 12 penny HDG common nails for your decking. If you predrill each nailing point, you will avoid splitting of board ends. Drive the nails at an angle as shown in figure 43-B. For deck screws and ring or spiral nails fasten straight down. Use three nails at board ends or joints and two at the middle joists.

• Place remaining decking and be sure to measure and maintain proper $3/16$" gap as you go. Set a 16 penny nail between the boards to ensure correct spacing. If your decking doesn't span the complete length of your deck, be sure to alternate the locations of decking joints. Straighten any warped boards with a chisel as shown in figures 43-C and 43-D. When you are 6 feet from placing the last board, begin to vary spacing slightly so that you can avoid ripping a board lengthwise to fit.

• When all the decking is in place, snap a chalk line along the outside face of the rim joists. Saw the deck boards at the chalk line so that they are flush with joists. See Figures 43-E and 43-F.

Lay Boards
Bark Side
Up

Figure 43-A

Drive Nails at
Opposite Angles

Figure 43-B

Use a Wood Chisel to
Straighten Warped Boards

Figure 43-C

Use a Wood Chisel to
Straighten Warped Boards

Figure 43-D

Trim Decking Boards by
Snapping a Chalk Line

Figure 43-E

Cut
Along
Chalkline
with a
Circular Saw

Figure 43-F

Measure as You Go

One difficulty you may experience while nailing down deck boards is keeping them parallel. You can solve this problem simply by measuring the distance remaining on the joists from time to time. Take measurements along both sides and the middle as shown below. Tack a string line a foot or two away to serve as a visual guide.

If you discover that some boards are uneven as you continue your work, make your correction gradually by adjusting the space between the next three or four boards.

When you have about six feet of decking left to place, begin adjusting board spacing to avoid an unsightly gap at the end of the deck.

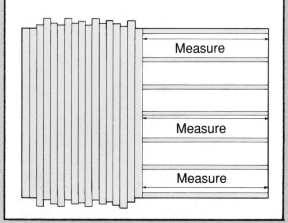

Measure

Measure

Measure

Deck Board Ties
For Installing Deck Boards
with NO Surface Nailing

1. Deck Board Tie

2. First Deck Board Fastened to Joist with Toenailing

3. Locator Prongs Positions Deck Tie for Nailing on Deck Board Edge

4. Slides Under Anchored Board

Courtesy of Simpson Strong-Tie Co., Inc.

Fitting Decking around Posts

• If you are extending your posts to use as railing members, you will have to notch decking boards to fit around the extended posts. You must remember to support specially cut deck boards at their ends with blocking or cleat support since typically joists will not occur at all the correct positions for nailing.

• Consult the illustrations below for methods of supporting decking around notched posts. Measure each side of the post allowing $3/16$" on each side as a drainage gap. Use your carpenter's square to mark these measurements on the decking.

• You can use either a power saw or a hand saw to make the two perpendicular cuts on your deck board. Next use a broad wood chisel to complete the notch. If you are especially handy with a power reciprocating saw, you can measure an oversize notch with arcs at the corners and use the saw to cut the entire notch in one operation.

• Be sure to nail decking properly to supporting joists or cleats around the post. Use 3 nails or 2 deck screws when you fasten decking to supports around the post. Predrill nails holes so that you don't split decking boards.

Post

Decking

Joist

Beam/Girder

2" x 4" Blocking

Post

Decking

Beam/Girder

2" x 4" Blocking

Joist

Post

Width of Notch Plus $3/16$"

Depth of Notch Plus $3/16$"

Cut Sides with Hand Saw or Power Saw

Notch Piece Out by Using a Chisel

Deck Board in Place

Railing Construction

• *Railings require careful planning before construction begins and should not be added as an afterthought.* Consult your local building department for code requirements on railing height, lateral strength, and baluster and rail spacing *before* you begin construction. Typical railing height is 36" from decking to the top of the cap rail.

• First consider if you want to extend deck posts through the decking as major railing supports or if you want to connect 4x4 posts to the rim joists on the perimeter of the deck. See the illustrations at the right for details on these two methods of railing construction.

• If you decide to use **attached post construction** rather than **extended post construction**, you must attach each post to the rim joist with at least two $^3/_8$" x 5" lag screws and washers at the bottom of the post. For a more finished look, you might want to bevel cut the end of the 4x4 below the screw heads. Predrill the lag screw holes in the post with a $^3/_8$" bit and don't put the holes in the beveled section of the post. Then place the post, checking for plumbness and marking the lag holes with a pencil. Drill these holes with a $^1/_4$" bit and secure the post firmly to the rim joist with lag screws and washers.

• Once your railing posts have been cut to the proper height, you will install the **cap rail** and other horizontal rail members. Cap rails are best constructed from either clear 2x4 or 2x6 boards laid flat. Mitre cap rails where they meet at right angles over a post as shown in the illustration at right. Use either a nailing cleat or a metal connector to make a secure connection between rail and post at points below the top of the 4x4.

• Toenail rails to posts with 10 penny HDG common nails or use 3" deck screws drilled at a slant. Whatever fastener you employ, don't skimp on quality here. There's nothing more disappointing than rusting fasteners bleeding down your railings and onto your deck surface.

• **Balusters** should be constructed from at least 2x2 material without knots that could make the baluster subject to breakage. Typical baluster spacing is either 6" or 8" on center depending upon local code requirements. Be sure to keep your balusters plumb and fasten at the top and bottom with either HDG 10 penny common nails or 2 $^1/_2$" deck screws which don't require predrilling. If you have beveled the bottom of your attached rail posts, you might want to bevel the tops and bottoms of your balusters for a unified look. If the balusters do not provide the main lateral strength for the rails, you can use finishing nails instead of common nails and then sink the nail heads with a nail punch and cover the heads with an exterior wood putty.

• Apply an appropriate wood finish to your completed railing, especially where the end grain of the wood is exposed on cap rails.

Extended Post Rail

Rail Post Bolted

Rail Connections

Mitre at Corner

Metal Anchor

Wood Blocking

Popular Railing Styles

2 x 6

2 x 2s

4 x 4 Post

2 x 4

1 x 1 Stops

2 x 4

2 x 2

2 x 2

Bench Construction

• The illustration below demonstrates one method of attached bench construction that can be added to an existing deck or built when you undertake new deck construction.

• There are as many bench options as you can imagine. However, a good guideline for bench construction is that the bench seat should be at least 18" high from the decking and at least 15" deep to provide comfortable seating. A bench with an integrated backrest can be designed to serve a dual purpose on high level decks where it functions as both a seat and a railing.

• No matter which bench design you select, you should use clear wood for bench seats which is free from knots, splitting, and other defects.

• To construct the bench shown below, fasten two 2x6 bench supports to decking with 12 gauge 8 1/4" long bench support brackets on both sides of the bench supports. Use 1/4" x 1 1/2" lag screws and washers to connect supports to brackets and brackets to decking.

• Following the dimensions shown below, cut the seat brace from 2x6 lumber. Secure the seat brace to the seat supports with 3/8" x 5 1/2" carriage bolts with nuts and washers.

• Next cut three 2x6's to the correct length and place flatwise on the bench supports. Use 10 penny HDG common nails or 3" deck screws to fasten bench seat boards to bench braces. Leave 1/4" spacing between seat boards for proper drainage. Secure 2x4 trim boards at front and back of bench.

Ready to Start Serious Planning?

Now that you have read this book from cover to cover, you're ready to start serious planning. As you can see, there are many details to consider, and they all tie together for successful completion of your deck project.

If the procedures appear at first confusing, reread the information outlined in this book several times before deciding which phases of construction you want to handle yourself and for which you might want to rely on professional assistance.

Because drawing up your own plan from scratch can be time consuming and difficult for the inexperienced builder, you might want to make planning and cost estimating easier by selecting a design from those shown in this book.

If blueprints with lumber lists are not immediately available from your building material dealer, you can order them by using the order form in the back of this book. If after reviewing the blueprints you still have questions, talk them over with your lumber dealer. Most dealers are familiar with construction and will be glad to help you.

The following 12 pages include an assortment of deck plans and deck-related accessories. Remember that construction blueprints can be obtained from your dealer or by using the order form on page 64. All blueprint plans include a complete material list, exterior elevations, sections and details, and step-by-step instructions for the successful completion of your deck project.

Example of a Typical Project Plan Sheet

Deck and Deck Accessory Plans

Complete Blueprint Plans are Available for All the Following Plans:

Design
B2062
Easy Deck

- Plans detailed for
  three deck sizes:
  8'wide x 12'deep
  12'wide x 12'deep
  12'wide x 16'deep
- Low cost construction
- Adaptable to all grades
- Can be built with standard lumber
- Large, professional easy-to-follow blueprints
- Complete list of materials
- Dimensional drawing of every detail

Design
B2002
Low Patio Deck

- Plans detailed for
  three deck sizes:
  12' wide x 12' deep
  16' wide x 12' deep
  20' wide x 12' deep
- Perfect for entertaining
- Built-in seating
- Adds value and beauty to your home
- Large, professional easy-to-follow blueprints
- Complete list of materials
- Dimensional drawing of every detail

Design
B2077

Hexagon Deck

- Overall Area 10' wide x 12' deep
- Free standing design
- Simple construction
- Two styles of railings
- Attractive design
- Large, professional easy-to-follow blueprints
- Complete list of materials
- Dimensional drawing of every detail

UCANDO Patterns
U00830

12' Octagon Deck or 12' Lookout

- Welcome to the best concept in tracing templates!
- No ruler—No measurements Just use the template.
- You can trace all parts and mark all hole locations to make one or more Octagon Decks. Assembly instructions included.
- Designed to go from ground level to 3' high with this material list. For heights above 3' consult your dealer.
- Detailed material list
- Easy to read instruction sheet
- Sturdy reuseable templates
- Cutting layout sheet

12' Lookout (add to present deck for a unique look)

12' Octagon Deck

Design
B2008
Raised Patio Deck

- Plans detailed for two deck sizes:
  12' wide x 12' deep
  16' wide x 12' deep
- Unique, attractive railed design
- Can be built at any height
- Fits any lot situation
- Simple construction
- Large, professional
  easy-to-follow blueprints
- Complete list of materials
- Dimensional drawing of
  every detail

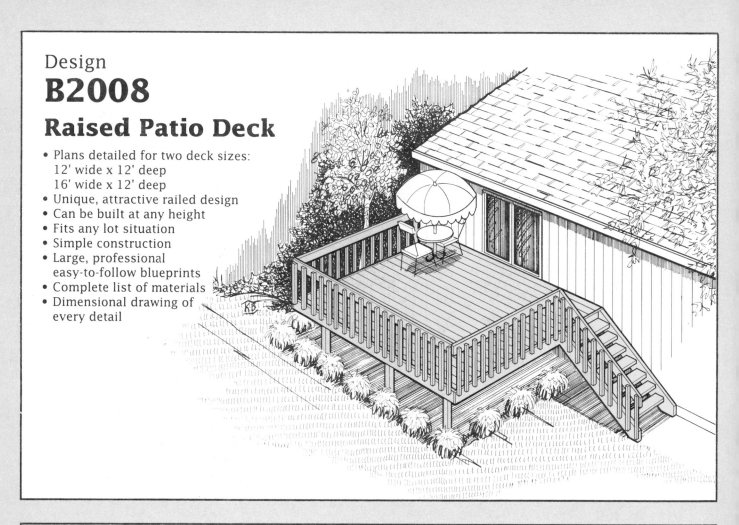

Design
B2076
Two Level Raised Deck

- Size:
  Overall area 20'wide x 22'deep
  Upper area 12'wide x 12'deep
  Lower area 18'wide x 12'deep
- Enhance the usefulness of
  your home
- Unique, attractive design
  with bench
- Can be built at any height
- Adaptable to any lot
  situation
- Large, professional
  easy-to-follow blueprints
- Complete list of materials
- Dimensional drawing of
  every detail

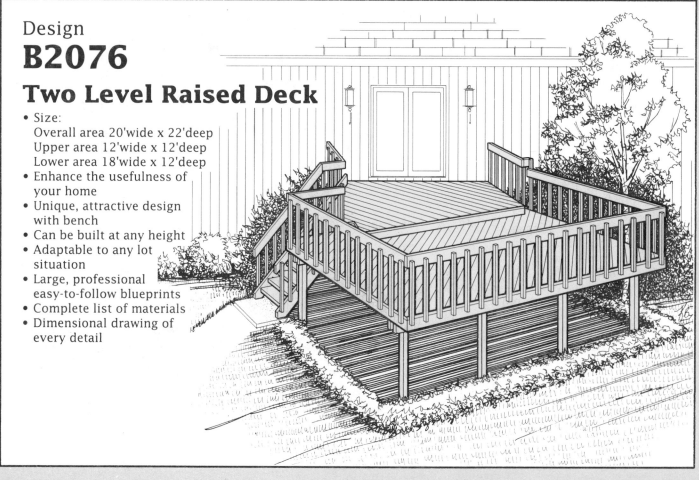

Design
B2057
Garden Deck

- Size:
  Total area: 12'wide x 19'deep
  Main deck: 12'wide x 16'deep
  with 8' x 8' plant/sun area.
- Unique design features decorative plant display area or sun deck
- Built-in seating
- Can be free standing or attached to your home
- Large, professional easy-to-follow blueprints
- Complete list of materials
- Dimensional drawing of every detail

Design
B2047
Two Level Deck

- Size:
  Total area: 14'wide x 15'deep
  Lower level: 8'wide x 8'deep
  Upper level: 12'wide x 9'deep
- Unique, attractive design features a two-level deck and bench
- Adds great value and usefulness to your home
- Simple construction
- Large, professional easy-to-follow blueprints
- Complete list of materials
- Dimensional Drawing of every detail

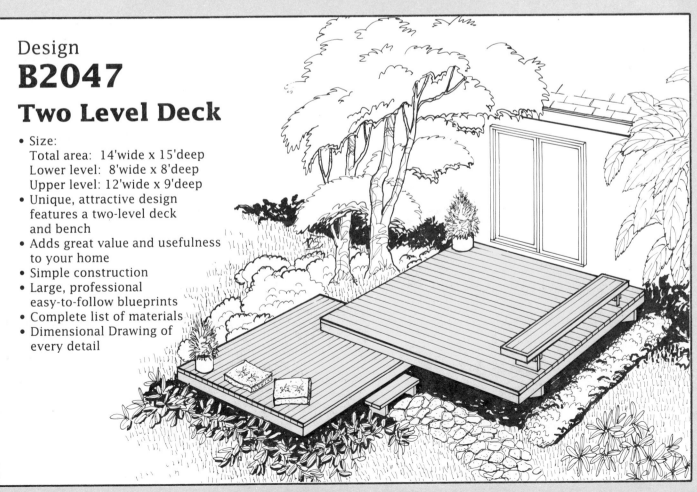

Design
B2058

High-Low Deck

- Size:
  Upper Level 8'wide x 10'deep
  Lower Level 15'-6"wide x 13'deep
- Designed as an add-on to an existing deck, or as a complete unit
- Features a unique conversation area, or optional fire pit
- Benches may be arranged as needed
- Can be stepped up or down
- Large, professional easy-to-follow blueprints
- Complete list of materials
- Dimensional drawing of every detail

Design
B2069

Split Level Deck

- Deck size:
  Total area 20'wide x 14'deep
  Upper level 12'wide x 12'deep
  Lower level 9'wide x 8'deep
- Low cost construction
- Acceptable to all grades
- Can be built with standard lumber

- Adds great value and usefulness to your home
- Large, professional easy-to-follow blueprints
- Complete list of materials
- Dimensional drawing of every detail

Design
B2075
Spa Deck

- Overall area 20'wide x 14'deep
  Lower level 10'wide x 14'deep
  Upper level 6'wide x 10'deep
- Designed for self-contained portable spas
- Convenient spa access
- Deck designed free standing or next to house

- Simple construction
- Spa plans not included
- Large, professional easy-to-follow blueprints
- Complete list of materials
- Dimensional drawing of every detail

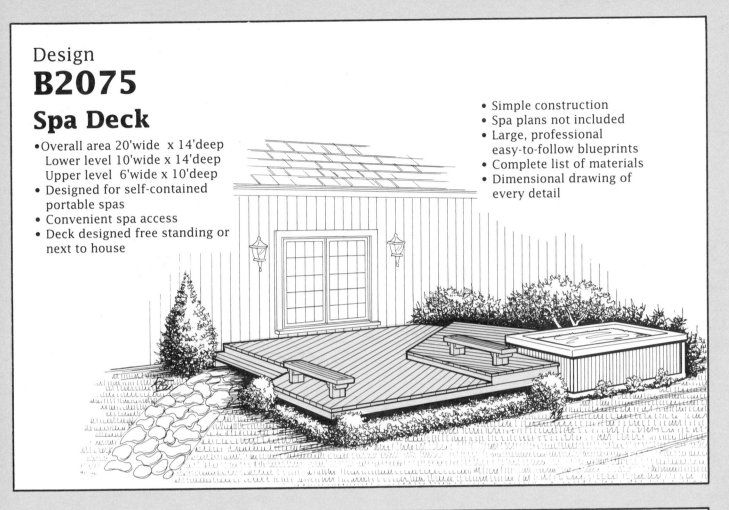

Design
B2030R
Pool Deck

- Party size deck:
  14' wide x 15' deep
- Can be built to fit any size pool
- Simple construction
- Large, professional easy-to-follow blueprints
- Complete list of materials
- Dimensional drawing of every detail

Design
B2055R
Shaded Deck

- Size:
  16'wide x 10'deep x 10' high
- Unique, attractive deck design features a sun screen covering
- Add value and beauty to your home
- Simple construction
- Perfect for entertaining
- Large, professional easy-to-follow blueprints
- Complete list of materials
- Dimensional drawing of every detail

Design
X6023
Screened Porch

- Size:
  12'wide x 16'deep
- Attractive addition to any home
- Large, professional easy-to-follow blueprints
- Complete list of materials
- Dimensional drawing of every detail

UCANDO Patterns
U00600
Stair Stringer

- Welcome to the best concept in tracing templates!
- Stair stringer tracing patterns may be used to build stringers for stair lengths from 2 to 15 (or more) steps
- A hard to find solution for building your own steps for decks and entryways
- Detailed material list
- Easy to read instruction sheet
- Sturdy reuseable templates
- Cutting layout sheet

Design
B2078
Deck Railings

- Five different railing styles
- Can be added to your existing deck
- Simple Construction
- Large, professional easy-to-follow blueprints
- Complete list of materials
- Dimensional drawing of every detail

Traditional 2" x 4"

Colonial

Contemporary Single Bevel

Traditional Square 2" x 2"

Contemporary Double Bevel

Design
B2066

Patio Cover

- Designed for two sizes: 12'wide x 12'deep or 16'wide x 12'deep
- Designed to cover an existing deck or patio, or may be used as a pavilion
- Unique design
- Free standing structure
- Can be built with standard lumber
- Simple construction
- Plan detailed with an alternate bench design
- Large, professional easy-to-follow blueprints
- Complete list of materials
- Dimensional drawing of every detail

Design
B2068

Easy Patio Cover

- Size 16'wide x 12'deep
- Unique attractive patio cover features a sun screen covering
- Add value and beauty to your home
- Simple construction
- Large, professional easy-to-follow blueprints
- Complete list of materials
- Dimensional drawing of every detail

Design
B2065
Deck Enhancements

- 4 Unique designs:
    Planter box : 3'-0" x 1'-7"
    Bench: 6'-0" x 1'-8"
    Decorative Screen: 6'-0" x 6'-0"
    End table: 2'-6" x 1'-2"
- Dresses up any existing deck
- Simple construction
- Can be free standing or attached to your deck
- Large, professional easy-to-follow blueprints
- Complete list of materials
- Dimensional drawing of every detail

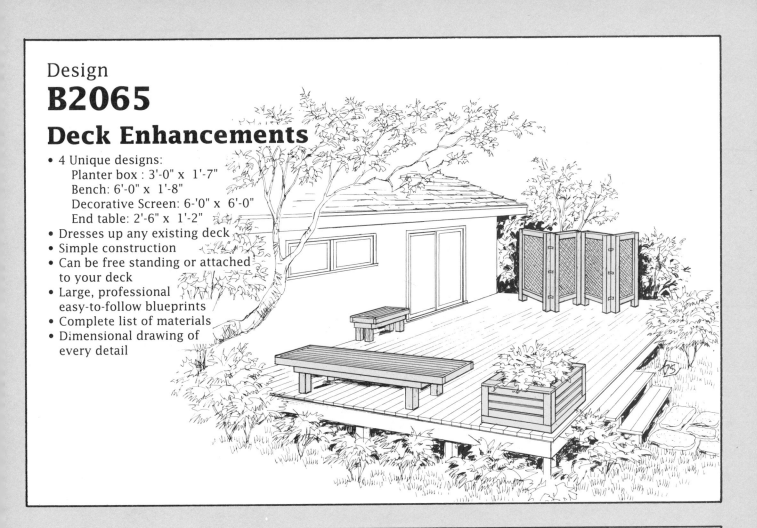

Design
B2029
Patio Furniture

- Three piece set
- Can be built with standard lumber
- Simple to build...doesn't even require power tools
- Large, professional easy-to-follow blueprints
- Complete list of materials
- Dimensional drawing of every detail

Design
B2049
PVC Outdoor Furniture

- Use plastic (PVC) pipe to build this chair and chaise lounge
- A project that's very practical and unique
- Simple construction...fun to do
- Use standard size cushions to complete your project
- Large, professional easy-to-follow blueprints
- Complete list of materials
- Dimensional drawing of every detail

UCANDO Patterns
U00702
Deck Rocker

- Welcome to a new concept in tracing templates!
  There is only one piece to handle. No loose pieces to get lost or a piece that is hard to find. From this one template you can trace all the parts and mark all the hole locations to make your deck rocker.
- Save up to 50% on your project!
- Detailed material list
- Easy to read instruction sheet
- Sturdy reuseable templates
- Cutting layout sheet

Design
B2070
Adirondack Lounge Chair

- A project that's very practical and unique
- Simple construction...fun to do
- Build it on a weekend
- Sturdy construction
- Two piece set
- Large, professional easy-to-follow blueprint
- Complete list of materials
- Dimensional drawing of every detail

Design
B2073
Leisure Bench with Table

- 5' long bench, seat height 17"
- 4' long table, table height 16"
- Simple construction
- Enhances your garden, patio, or deck
- Complements any setting
- Large, professional easy-to-follow blueprints
- Complete list of materials
- Dimensional drawing of every detail

Design
B2048
Barbeque Cart

- Stands 36" high with 39" x 25½" countertop...with side shelf for cooking items...total length: 51"
- A must for your outdoor cooking
- Easy to build with standard lumber and materials
- Large, professional easy-to-follow blueprints
- Complete list of materials
- Dimensional drawing of every detail

Design
B2032
Fences and Gates

- 9 different designs to select
- How to estimate
- How to buy
- How to build
- From wood to chain link fencing basics
- Ideas for security-privacy-beauty
- Necessary materials & tools
- D-I-Y tips & instructions
- Large, professional easy-to-follow blueprints
- Complete list of materials
- Dimensional drawing of every detail

Design
B2003

Picnic King Bench and Table

- Converts from table to bench
- Sturdy construction
- Build it on a weekend
- Easy to follow plan
- Wood cutting diagrams to help you cut costs
- Large, professional easy-to-follow blueprints
- Complete list of materials
- Dimensional drawing of every detail

UCANDO Patterns
U00700

Hexagon Picnic Table

- Welcome to a new concept in tracing templates! There is only one piece to handle. No loose pieces to get lost or a piece that is hard to find. From this one template you can trace all the parts and mark all the hole locations to make your hexagon table.
- Save up to 50% on your project!
- Detailed material list
- Easy to read instruction sheet
- Sturdy reuseable templates
- Cutting layout sheet

Design
B2051R

Picnic Tables

- These sturdy picnic tables are ideal for backyard barbeques
- Choose from two designs:
  Rectangular shape - 60" x 72" x 30"high
  Octagon shape - 56" x 56" x 30"high
- Sturdy construction...will last for years
- Build it on a weekend
- Large, professional easy-to-follow blueprints
- Complete list of materials
- Dimensional drawing of every detail

UCANDO Patterns
U00740

Portable Folding Table and Bench Set

- Welcome to the best concept in tracing templates! Noruler - No measurements - just usethe template. You can trace all parts and mark all hole locations to make your Portable Folding Table. Assembly instructions included.
- Nut, bolt & screw construction
- Light weight
- Built in carrying handle
- Benches store inside table
- Detailed material list
- Easy to read instruction sheet
- Sturdy reuseable templates
- Cutting layout sheet

Design
B2074

Gazebo, 6-Sided

- 9'-2"wide x 8'-0"deep
- Unique, attractive design that will complement either your home or garden
- Cutting templates for rafters and center post
- Add value and beauty to your home
- Simple construction
- Large, professional easy-to-follow blueprints
- Complete list of materials
- Dimensional drawing of every detail

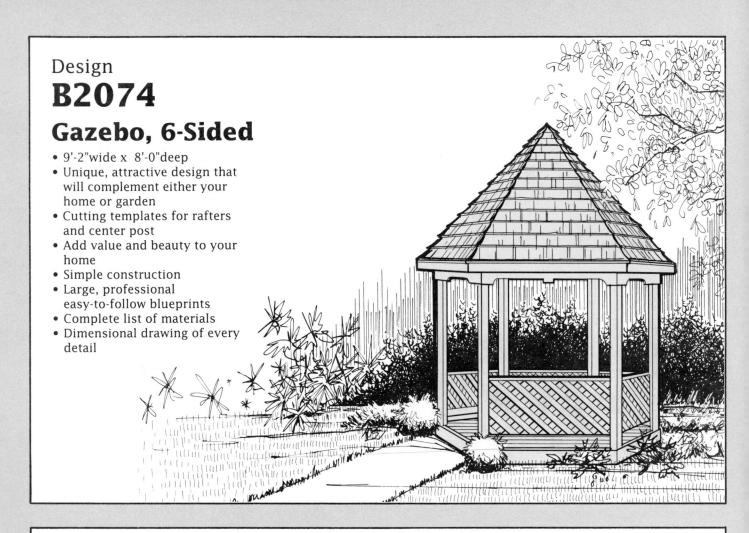

UCANDO Patterns
U00888

12' Gazebo

- Welcome to the best concept in tracing templates! There is only one piece to handle. No loose pieces to get lost or a piece that is hard to find. From this one template you can trace all the parts and mark all the hole locations to make your 12' Gazebo.
- Save up to 50% on your project!
- Detailed material list
- Easy to read instruction sheet
- Sturdy reuseable templates
- Cutting layout sheet

UCANDO® PROJECT PLANS

All plans are easy-to-follow and fully detailed. A complete list of material included.

B2056   13'x13'x10' high
Wooden Swings

B2041   8' x 8'
Jungle Gym

B2072   8' x 8'
Garden Entryway

B2067   Canopy 12'-0" x 5'-0" x 7'6"
Bench 6'-0" Long
Garden Swing

B2061   10' x 10'
Contemporary   12' x 10'
Garden Shed   14' x 10'

B2064   10' x 6'
Log Storage Shed

B2071   6'-0" x 6'-0" x 7'2"
Children's Playhouse

B2025
Two Doghouses

B2042   12' x 12' x 11'10"
Storage Shed   12' x 16' x 11'10"
   12' x 20' x 11'10"

B2004   8' x 8' x 8'2"
Storage Barn   12' x 8' x 8'2"
   16' x 8' x 8'2"

B2059   8' x 8'
Gable Storage   8' x 10'
Shed   8' x 12'

B2054   12' x 8' x 9'4"
Storage   12' x 12' x 9'4"
Shed   12' x 16' x 9'4"

A100—PROJECT PLANS—contains more than 155 do-it-yourself projects you can build—includes garages, gazebos, decks, storage sheds, pole buildings, horse barns, furniture and children's projects.

BLUEPRINT ORDER FORM

•When you're ready to order construction blueprints we recommend that you order them from the dealer who provided this book.

•Your dealer can give you valuable and cost-saving information about local building code requirements and the availablity of local contractors and financing should you so require.

•Take advantage of your dealer's knowledge and experience!

BLUEPRINT ORDER FORM

NATIONAL PLAN SERVICE USA, INC.
DEPT. A200
P.O. BOX 66973
CHICAGO, IL 60666-0973
PHONE TOLL FREE 1-800-533-4350 IN ILLINOIS 708-833-0640 FAX ORDER 1-800-344-4293

ALL PRICES SUBJECT TO CHANGE WITHOUT NOTICE   NOT RETURNABLE

PLEASE RUSH ME THE ITEMS CHECKED BELOW

☐ A100	Book	$ 4.95	☐ B2041	Gym	$ 5.95	☐ B2057	Deck	$ 5.95	☐ B2068	Cover	$ 5.95	☐ B2077	Deck	$ 5.95
☐ B2002	Deck	$ 5.95	☐ B2042	Shed	$ 5.95	☐ B2058	Deck	$ 5.95	☐ B2069	Deck	$ 5.95	☐ B2078	Railings	$ 5.95
☐ B2003	Table	$ 5.95	☐ B2047	Deck	$ 5.95	☐ B2059	Shed	$ 5.95	☐ B2070	Chair	$ 5.95	☐ U00600	Stringer	$ 5.95
☐ B2004	Shed	$ 5.95	☐ B2048	Cart	$ 5.95	☐ B2061	Shed	$ 5.95	☐ B2071	Playhouse	$ 5.95	☐ U00700	Table	$10.95
☐ B2008	Deck	$ 5.95	☐ B2049	Furniture	$ 5.95	☐ B2062	Deck	$ 5.95	☐ B2072	Entryway	$ 5.95	☐ U00702	Rocker	$ 6.95
☐ B2025	Dog House	$ 5.95	☐ B2051R	Table	$ 5.95	☐ B2064	Shed	$ 5.95	☐ B2073	Bench	$ 5.95	☐ U00740	Bench	$ 8.95
☐ B2029	Furniture	$ 5.95	☐ B2054	Shed	$ 5.95	☐ B2065	Enhancements	$ 5.95	☐ B2074	Gazebo	$ 5.95	☐ U00830	Deck	$14.95
☐ B2030R	Deck	$ 5.95	☐ B2055R	Deck	$ 5.95	☐ B2066	Covers	$ 5.95	☐ B2075	Deck	$ 5.95	☐ U00888	Gazebo	$14.95
☐ B2032	Fences	$ 5.95	☐ B2056	Swing	$ 5.95	☐ B2067	Swing	$ 5.95	☐ B2076	Deck	$ 5.95	☐ X6023	Porch	$12.95

☐ Payment is enclosed (check or money order)
☐ Please charge to my credit card below
SALES TAX Illinois Residents please add **7%** sales tax.

USE CREDIT CARDS ONLY FOR $10.00 OR MORE—U.S. ONLY

MasterCard ☐ If you wish to use your charge card, check box at left and fill out boxes below.
Expiration Date
VISA ☐ Month/Year_____

Credit Card No._____

TOTAL . . . . $_____
TAX (see tax note) . . . . $_____
Shipping & Handling charges . . $ 2.00 _____
TOTAL ORDER . . . . $_____

Name_____
Address_____
City_____ State_____ Zip_____
Phone (   ) _____

BLUEPRINT ORDER FORM

NATIONAL PLAN SERVICE USA, INC.
DEPT. A200
P.O. BOX 66973
CHICAGO, IL 60666-0973
PHONE TOLL FREE 1-800-533-4350 IN ILLINOIS 708-833-0640 FAX ORDER 1-800-344-4293

ALL PRICES SUBJECT TO CHANGE WITHOUT NOTICE   NOT RETURNABLE

PLEASE RUSH ME THE ITEMS CHECKED BELOW

☐ A100	Book	$ 4.95	☐ B2041	Gym	$ 5.95	☐ B2057	Deck	$ 5.95	☐ B2068	Cover	$ 5.95	☐ B2077	Deck	$ 5.95
☐ B2002	Deck	$ 5.95	☐ B2042	Shed	$ 5.95	☐ B2058	Deck	$ 5.95	☐ B2069	Deck	$ 5.95	☐ B2078	Railings	$ 5.95
☐ B2003	Table	$ 5.95	☐ B2047	Deck	$ 5.95	☐ B2059	Shed	$ 5.95	☐ B2070	Chair	$ 5.95	☐ U00600	Stringer	$ 5.95
☐ B2004	Shed	$ 5.95	☐ B2048	Cart	$ 5.95	☐ B2061	Shed	$ 5.95	☐ B2071	Playhouse	$ 5.95	☐ U00700	Table	$10.95
☐ B2008	Deck	$ 5.95	☐ B2049	Furniture	$ 5.95	☐ B2062	Deck	$ 5.95	☐ B2072	Entryway	$ 5.95	☐ U00702	Rocker	$ 6.95
☐ B2025	Dog House	$ 5.95	☐ B2051R	Table	$ 5.95	☐ B2064	Shed	$ 5.95	☐ B2073	Bench	$ 5.95	☐ U00740	Bench	$ 8.95
☐ B2029	Furniture	$ 5.95	☐ B2054	Shed	$ 5.95	☐ B2065	Enhancements	$ 5.95	☐ B2074	Gazebo	$ 5.95	☐ U00830	Deck	$14.95
☐ B2030R	Deck	$ 5.95	☐ B2055R	Deck	$ 5.95	☐ B2066	Covers	$ 5.95	☐ B2075	Deck	$ 5.95	☐ U00888	Gazebo	$14.95
☐ B2032	Fences	$ 5.95	☐ B2056	Swing	$ 5.95	☐ B2067	Swing	$ 5.95	☐ B2076	Deck	$ 5.95	☐ X6023	Porch	$12.95

☐ Payment is enclosed (check or money order)
☐ Please charge to my credit card below
SALES TAX Illinois Residents please add **7%** sales tax.

USE CREDIT CARDS ONLY FOR $10.00 OR MORE—U.S. ONLY

MasterCard ☐ If you wish to use your charge card, check box at left and fill out boxes below.
Expiration Date
VISA ☐ Month/Year_____

Credit Card No._____

TOTAL . . . . $_____
TAX (see tax note) . . . . $_____
Shipping & Handling charges . . $ 2.00 _____
TOTAL ORDER . . . . $_____

Name_____
Address_____
City_____ State_____ Zip_____
Phone (   ) _____

YOU MAY PHOTOCOPY THIS ORDER FORM